T0156672

THE LAST DAY'S
SPIRITUAL SURVIVAL GUIDE

BRUCE A SHERBOURNE

But Jesus looked at *them* and said to them, "With men this is impossible, but with God all things are possible." (Matthew 19:26)

WESTBOW
PRESS®
A DIVISION OF THOMAS NELSON
& ZONDERVAN

WestBow Press books may be ordered through booksellers or by contacting:

WestBow Press
A Division of Thomas Nelson & Zondervan
1663 Liberty Drive
Bloomington, IN 47403
www.westbowpress.com
1 (866) 928-1240

ISBN: 978-1-4908-6756-4 (sc)
ISBN: 978-1-4908-6757-1 (hc)
ISBN: 978-1-4908-6755-7 (e)

Library of Congress Control Number: 2015901300

Print information available on the last page.

WestBow Press rev. date: 03/01/2016

"The Last Days Spiritual Survival Guide embraces a straightforward empowering form of commutating clearly to the reader the vital need to make life's most critical decision with infallible urgency. Interwoven with the gospel according to Jesus is Bruce's true life story that reveals the divine power of God saving a man through the darkest depths of painful test, tribulation and deep suffering.

Moreover, it contains a vast wealth of practical spiritual survival strategies to overcome your own personal tribulation. In addition, the book is packed full of valuable material, resources, and a wealth of prayers, Bible promises, essential Psalms, and proven methods and study's to help you overcome test, trials, and tribulations.

Together, these custom tailored truths and teachings are tactically designed to lead the reader into a genuine relationship with Jesus, salvation and serve as an essential guide in growing the faith of believers and nonbelievers a like." Bruce A. Sherbourne

Matthew 24: 32-42.

"Now learn a lesson from the fig tree. When its branches bud and its leaves begin to sprout, you know that summer is near. In the same way, when you see all these things, you can know his return is very near, right at the door. I tell you the truth, this generation will not pass from the scene until all these things take place. Heaven and earth will disappear, but my words will never disappear.

"However, no one knows the day or hour when these things will happen, not even the angels in heaven or the Son himself. Only the Father knows.

"When the Son of Man returns, it will be like it was in Noah's day. In those days before the flood, the people were enjoying banquets and parties and weddings right up to the time Noah entered his boat. People didn't realize what was going to happen until the flood came and swept them all away. That is the way it will be when the Son of Man comes. "Two men will be working together in the field; one will be taken, the other left. Two women will be grinding flour at the mill; one will be taken, the other left. "So you, too, must keep watch! For you don't know what day your Lord is coming." Jesus Christ

Contents

Cover Story and Introduction

The Cover picture was taken in Israel on the Mount of Olives-Dominus Flevit Church-shaped of Tears where Jesus wept for Jerusalem."

But as he came closer to Jerusalem and saw the city ahead, he began to weep. "How I wish today that you of all people would understand the way to peace. But now it is hidden from your eyes. Luke 19: 41-42. This book has been written to open your eyes to the reality that Jesus is the One and only living God and he is returning to take His rightful position as Lord of His earthly kingdom very soon.

The Spirit of the Sovereign Lord is upon me, for the Lord has anointed me to bring good news to the poor. He has sent me to comfort the broken hearted and to proclaim that captives will be released and prisoners will be freed. He has sent me to tell those who mourn that the time of the Lords favor has come and with it, the day of God's anger against their enemies. Isaiah 1: 1-2. Jesus fulfilled verse one 2000 years ago; He will fulfill verse two during the tribulation.

You must warn each other every day, while it is still "Today," so that none of you will be deceived by sin and hardened against God. For if we are faithful to the end, trusting God just as firmly as when we first believed, we will share in all that belongs to Christ. Remember what it says:

"Today when you hear his voice, don't harden your hearts as Israel did when they rebelled."

If you don't know what to say just say "Jesus." There is power in the name. Before reading this book, acknowledge God and thank Him for reaching out to touch your heart with His amazing grace.

Cover photo taken by Bruce Sherbourne in 2007.

My Deepest Appreciation to...

My precious mom, who believed in me and this message enough to support me while I sought the Lord's heart concerning letting go of everything to obey this special call. Most important, my sincere gratitude to my mom's devotion and love in the face of indescribable challenges. From the time of my birth she has been my most cherished friend and a genuine image bearer of our Lord Jesus. I dedicate this book to you and I pray that our Father will richly bless you throughout all eternity for you faithfulness and love.

My step father Ron, who has laid down his life faithfully to obey God's call to pray for me and to provide for me during my many tribulations.

A special thanks to Mark Battiato who is my brother in Christ and most cherished friend. Thank you, Mark for supporting me, praying for me, and loving me, in spite of me.

My daughter Aubrielle "Peanut" who proves that child like faith can move mountains. Thank you Aubrielle Joy for allowing Jesus to touch my heart with His love through you in extraordinary ways. You truly are one of Jesus' faithful ones. And I thank my son Dawson for reflecting the kindness and love of our Lord. Each of my addtional children Mikayla, Landon, Karlie, and Eliana have helped to bring the passion of Christ's truth to this book to the hearts of those in tribulation.

My sister Cheryl and her husband Randy and their children Grant, Victoria, and little Gianna. Sometimes Jesus simply shines through our loved ones lives' to bring healing during our personal tribulations. You're all very precious to me.

CHAPTER 1

The Gospel of Jesus Christ

The greatness of God assures the worth of humankind. God, the all-powerful Creator, cares for His most valuable creation—people.

If you're reading this book, you may come to realize that you need to draw near to God in this critical hour before His near return, or you may be reading this as a person who was left behind at the rapture. In either case this book has been custom designed for you to discover Christ and what it means to truly trust in Him for life.

As frightening as the reality of being left behind at the rapture is, please understand that there is still hope in a genuine relationship with Jesus Christ. The age of the church will pass away. The Holy Spirit, however, is still reaching out to all those who are willing to repent and to believe the gospel of Jesus Christ. My purpose in writing this book is to help you to see the saving grace of God and to extend an invitation to you to experience the revelation of Jesus Christ and His divine offer of salvation.

Believing in Jesus now is what you need more than anything. The gospel is the joyous good news that because of God's great love for humankind, He sent His Son, Jesus Christ, to die on the cross and to pay the penalty for our sins, dying as a substitute in our place. This is the only way a holy and just God could declare sinners not guilty. God then raised Jesus from the dead to demonstrate the full acceptability of this sacrifice. To reap the benefit of what Christ Jesus did—to become "born again" and receive God's Holy Spirit—you must personally place faith in Christ the Savior.

It is essential that you now seek God with all of your heart as you journey through these pages. The stakes are high, and the coming judgment is nothing short of a seven-year period of hell on earth, followed by the final judgment of all the unsaved, who will face eternal separation from God in a place of great suffering. To say the least, you face the most critical decision you'll ever make regarding your eternal destiny. It is vital that you turn to Jesus Christ as your Savior and Lord, and you must call upon His name for mercy now.

Believe that God loves all human beings, including you, immensely. Never forget that. God made humans as social beings. We were not created to be alone. We were created to enter into and enjoy relationships with others. The most important relationship we were created to enter into is that with God Himself. There is a hunger in the heart of people to be close to God Himself. There is a hunger in the heart of people for purpose and forgiveness that none but God can satisfy. It is a vacuum that only God can fill. Human beings were created with a need for fellowship with God.

The problem that may cause you or has caused you to be left behind is sin, or, more precisely, the sin of unbelief, which can be defined as willful suppression of the truth. Human sin is pervasive. Jesus taught that both external acts and inner thoughts render a person guilty before God. This is a critical truth, because no matter how good you thought you were, the issue was never about simply being good. In order to be guiltless before a holy and perfect God, you must be perfect, and there is the problem: only one man is perfect. And the greater problem is that we have rebelled against God because we are born into this world with our backs to God and our eyes blinded by the poison of pride. Consequently, it is now human nature to do over and over again what comes naturally. We sin, and then we try to avoid both God and our guilt. This is why you will not be raptured with the church. You have yet to turn to God from your life of independence and sin to face the issue of sin, namely by confessing that you know you need to turn to Jesus as the Lord of your life, but you willfully refuse to do it so you can be the god of your life. We do this to avoid the narrow path that requires us to deny our selfish nature and to surrender to living to please Jesus instead of ourselves. We all know deep in our hearts that there is a cost for doing what is righteous or right in this fallen world. The Scriptures tell us that most people are unwilling to do what it takes:

> You can enter God's Kingdom only through the narrow gate. The highway to hell is broad, and its gate is wide for the many who choose that

3

way. But the gateway to life is very narrow and the road is difficult, and only a few ever find it. (Matthew 7:13–14)

Why is it so difficult? Mainly we find it so because of the sin of unbelief. We don't really believe the truth of God's Word in our hearts. Instead, we create our own homemade version of what God is like, and in so doing, we remain in our sin, believing a lie. The world system that Satan designed is one both of empty promises and of great temptation. The broad highway to hell that Jesus warns about clearly refers to the reality that, given a free will, the majority of people will take the path that seems to offer the greatest amount of instant gratification and the least amount of effort. Satan works to distort healthy desires into addictions and bondage. So, to answer the question about why so many reject submitting to Jesus as Lord, we can say it is because submission requires a complete commitment, with the willingness to let go of all your dreams and ambitions and to live for His. This radical commitment that may call us to die for our Lord is only possible through God's grace and the gift of faith initiated from heaven and applied through the gift of the Holy Spirit.

Jesus says, "For no one can come to me unless the Father who sent me draws them to me, and at the last day I will raise them up" (John 6:44). God will come to you through His Holy Spirit, through teachers, preachers, books, creation, and even angels in some cases, to bring you both the revelation of your true condition apart from Him in the face of the coming judgment and also the revelation of the gospel of Christ Jesus' love for you. Most of us pass up this invitation around seven times before we repent. The lure of riches and prosperity in the material world is very powerful and gains its strength from our nature being vulnerable, despite its roots in the poison of Satan's pride. I would like to make it very clear to you that God's mercy, grace, and love for you are greater than your deepest sin.

Paul the apostle said,

> I thank Christ Jesus our Lord, who has given me strength to do his work. He considered me trustworthy and appointed me to serve him, even though I used to blaspheme the name of Christ. In my insolence, I persecuted his people. But God had mercy on me because I did it in ignorance and unbelief. Oh, how generous and gracious our Lord was! He filled me with the faith and love that come from Christ Jesus. (1 Timothy 1:12–14)

For many of us, prior to being born again, we are sinning continually in ignorance and unbelief, just like Paul. As the writer of 1 Timothy reminds us,

> This is a trustworthy saying, and everyone should accept it: "Christ Jesus came into the world to save sinners"—and I am the worst of them all. But God had mercy on me so that Christ Jesus could use me as a prime example of his great patience with even the worst sinners. Then others will realize that they, too, can believe in him and receive eternal life. All honor and glory to

> God forever and ever! He is the eternal King, the unseen one who never dies; he alone is God. Amen. (1 Timothy 1:15–17)

As we dig deeper into the origin of our condition as sinners, keep in mind that God is saving sinners. There is only one unforgivable sin, and that is to refuse to deal with the Holy Spirit's many convictions of your need for salvation and a pardon from sin's penalty of death. You can willfully suppress the truth of the Holy Spirit of God to the point that your heart will harden and ultimately die, ending up unable to receive or hear the voice of God.

Let's look at how deep this issue of the sin of unbelief and ignorance has become. Two thousand years ago, God came to the earth He created with a very specific mission. He came to save us all of us whom He had known through foreknowledge would live His way. Most people up to this day are blind to their need for a Savior. Scripture reveals the answer why:

> But the people's minds were hardened, and to this day whenever the old covenant is being read, the same veil covers their minds so they cannot understand the truth. And this veil can be removed only by believing in Christ. Yes, even today when they read Moses' writings, their hearts are covered with that veil and they do not understand. *But whenever someone turns to the Lord, the veil is taken away. For the Lord is the Spirit, and wherever the Spirit of the Lord is, there is freedom.* So all of us who have had that veil removed can see

and reflect the glory of the Lord. And the Lord—
who is the Spirit—makes us more and more like
him as we are changed into his glorious image. (2
Corinthians 3:14–15, emphasis added)

We begin to assume that everything is about us and about our pursuit of happiness and pleasure. In reality, when we remain blind to the true purpose of life, there is a deadly power at work both inside and outside of humanity that leads to eternal destruction. What could be so awful as to cause this blindness to our guilt in sin without really being detected?

Let's go back to the beginning and consider the origin of sin. The need for redemption began long ago when our first ancestors were given a choice. Adam and Eve were the perfect candidates to pass the test, yet "When the Old Serpent, he who had been cast out of heaven for his pride, whose whole nature as devil was pride, spoke his words of temptation into the ear of Eve, these words carried with them the very poison of hell. And when she listened and yielded her desire and her will to the prospect of being as God, knowing both good and evil, the poison entered into her soul and blood and life, destroying that blessed humility and dependence upon God which would have been our everlasting happiness. And instead of this, her life and the life of the race that sprang from her became corrupted to its very root, with the most terrible of all sins and curses, the poison of Satan's own pride." Quote from Andrew Murray's book titled "Humility The Beauty of Holiness", published by Anson D.F. Randolph &

Co. 1985. pg: 17–18. Pride made redemption needful. You see, once the poison of Satan's pride entered mankind, God's Holy Spirit departed. We lost the Holy Spirit at the fall of mankind, and if we remain without it—if we willfully suppress the truth that we need it and try to avoid God and not face our guilt—we will miss the very purpose for which we were created, namely to have a personal relationship with God. It is impossible to know God without having received His Holy Spirit.

God's heart is full of grace. Despite mankind's alienation and rebellion, God reached out to us with His wonderful grace and provided a way of salvation. The word *grace* means undeserved favor. Scripture tells us that salvation is a grace gift and cannot be earned. We cannot attain it by good performance because God's infinite standards would require us to be perfect. Ephesians 2:8–9 affirms this: "By grace you have been saved, through faith and this is not of yourselves, it is the gift of God not by works so that no one can boast." While salvation is a free gift to us, the incalculable price God paid for it was the death of His own Son on the cross. There is no way words could ever describe the cost of our salvation. Jesus, who was fully man and fully God, took the punishment on Himself. What did this punishment involve? Though God's love motivated Him to want to save us, His absolute holiness demanded that sin be punished. This means that God loved us so much that He sent Jesus to bear the penalty for our sins! Since the Scriptures declare, "For the wages of sin is death, but the free gift of God is eternal life through Christ Jesus our Lord," Romans 6:23. Jesus would have to taste death or hell for each one of us to offer us the free gift of eternal life.

Once you realize that you are alienated from God by the poison of Satan's pride and resulting sin, you will recognize your true need and your personal ungodliness in the face of God. This can be a very painful realization that pierces the heart, but the good news is that it was for the very purpose of dying for your personal sins that Jesus came into the world. It is easy for us to discount the seriousness of Jesus' sacrificial death because we feel as if we didn't kill Him, yet in reality we all are responsible for Jesus' death and suffering because He came to bear the penalty for every sin ever committed by mankind, past, present, and future. That means that in reality we are just as guilty as those Romans who nailed Him to the cross or the Pharisees and Sadducees who condemned Him to death.

Jesus did more than pay the penalty for sin for all mankind; as a result of His resurrection, He settled the question once and for all as to whether there was life after death. In the verse above He declared, "I am the resurrection." What this means to you and me is that all who are in Christ and are trusting Christ for life will live eternally in heaven with Him. The other side of the coin is that as we move away from His invitation, our hearts will grow cold and harden. Eventually we will no longer hear His call of redemption, and this is called blasphemy of the Holy Spirit.

If we move away from the gospel of Jesus, it's because we are unwilling to obey God and surrender to His way of life. In essence, we willfully suppress the truth of the gospel of Christ so we can be our own god while we live a self-centered life instead of God centered. Remember, this is the broad way that most choose because following Jesus means denying our natural self-centered nature and requires us to submit to God's will whatever the cost. True belief is a total commitment to turn your life over to God's will. This path of life is narrow according to Scripture:

> You can enter God's Kingdom only through the narrow gate. The highway to hell is broad, and its gate is wide for the many who choose that way. But the gateway to life is very narrow and the road is difficult, and only a few ever find it. (Matthew 7:13–14)

The gateway that leads to eternal life requires God's help to find and enter. This help is the gift of God's Holy Spirit. To be born again means to believe in the gospel of Jesus and to receive the Holy Spirit in faith.

In order to return to God, you must turn to God's Word because faith comes from hearing the Word of God. I will do my best to reveal the truth of the gospel found in God's Word to provide you with an opportunity to repent and give you an invitation to join Jesus and the family of God in eternity. Jesus is the only friend who is willing to enter into the depths of the darkness of the tribulation through His Spirit to lead you out of certain judgment into salvation, so please humble yourselves and forget your past beliefs. As difficult as it may be, it is now time to forget the view you have held of reality or religion. It is time to change your worldview and open you heart and mind to a revelation of Christ Jesus from the Holy Spirit. Today, you have a choice before you—to follow the broad way, the way of the masses, the way of delusion, or to turn to the narrow path of truth regarding the living Savior Christ Jesus, who is calling you home through this invitation.

There may be no immediate way out of the tribulation, but you can invite the divine power of God's presence to enter your heart, and He will provide all you need to enter heaven's gate. In order to do this, you may have to accept the revelation that you may have deceived yourself. You may have to surrender long-held beliefs or habits that you cling to, and you will have to be willing to give your life genuinely to God, who saves us from sin and death. The way to heaven begins with a choice. As Paul wrote to the Romans,

> So since God's grace has set us free from the law, does this mean we can go on sinning? Of course not! Don't you realize that whatever you choose to obey becomes your master? You can choose sin, which leads to death, or you can choose to obey God and receive his approval. (Romans 6:16)

It is very likely that many of you who are reading this believed a lie and either thought you were obeying God when in fact you were not or just didn't believe the whole gospel story and elected to live a life independent of God. Either way you have a second chance, and I am writing this invitation to you because God loves you profoundly and is a God of second chances. Read this book and discover the love that reaches out to forgive your sins and save you from judgment and punishment in hell.

If we push away from the truth, we give authority to Satan, who is the outside force that works to tempt your prideful nature into sin. In a sense we deceive ourselves into believing a lie so we can deny the truth and live for ourselves. We end up believing that there will be no penalty or judgment awaiting us at death. Scripture clearly refutes this lie:

> They will be condemned at the time of judgment.
> Sinners will have no place among the godly. For
> the LORD watches over the path of the godly,
> but the path of the wicked leads to destruction.
> (Psalm 1:5–6)

At this point I hope it is beginning to become clearer as to why the good news of Jesus' gift demands a response. You must either believe or disbelieve in Jesus Christ, the Savior who died on the cross. You cannot hear this gospel of Jesus and remain neutral. You are either moved toward belief or away from it. To believe Jesus has ransomed you in reality means you believe that you're guilty and headed for judgment and that God is a God of pardon and has issued many a pardon from His heavenly court throughout all time, sealed with the blood of Jesus, signed in the Father's name. I hope you're beginning to understand that salvation is initiated from above, as the Scriptures declare:

For no one can come to me unless the Father who sent me draws them to me, and at the last day I will raise them up. As it is written in the Scriptures, "They will all be taught by God." Everyone who listens to the Father and learns from him comes to me. John 6:44-45.

God is a God of second chances, and He is calling you to Jesus right now during these final years of life as we know it to turn from the power of Satan and sin and turn to Him, to live for Him.

For even the Son of Man came not to be served but to serve others and to give his life as a ransom for many. (Matthew 20:28)

CHAPTER 2

Receiving the Gospel Truth

The root question is, "Are you willing to believe and repent and be baptized for the remission of your sins and then trust Christ to help you love God and your fellowman by living to please Christ Jesus instead of yourself?" When we consider what Christ has done, it is the goodness of God that draws us to repentance. I really want to help you understand what true repentance looks like. True repentance is coming to a full realization that we have rebelled against our Maker—against His way and His righteous law.

When we turn to God, He initiates the gift of faith and repentance from above, and it results in a complete about-face from disobedience toward God to obedience, love, and cooperation with Him. It means that we come to abhor ourselves for our self-willed, rebellious, sinful past. The time of repentance is the crisis of your life. It is the turning point in your entire destiny. It opens our hearts to receive the Holy Spirit, which is our comforter, guide, teacher, and instructor. When God's Spirit enters man, he is born again, and the Scriptures declare, "This means that anyone who belongs to Christ has become a new person. The old life is gone; a new life has begun!" (2 Corinthians 5:17).

When we are finally brought to real repentance, we are new creations. We are ready, in every phase of our lives, to say, "Yes, Lord. Your will be done." In real repentance, we become completely sick and tired of our own selfish ways. We are truly sorry for our sins—and we are ready and willing to make a permanent change. We are now ready to turn around and go the other way—*God's* way. At this point our Creator can begin the process of creating spiritual character in us. This happens as a result of His Holy Spirit being placed in us.

> So now there is no condemnation for those who belong to Christ Jesus. And because you belong to him, the power of the life-giving Spirit has freed you from the power of sin that leads to death. (Romans 5:1–2)

Before we trusted Christ Jesus, the Scriptures declare we lived according to the flesh and those who live by the flesh are drawing solely on their human resources. This takes place in areas like thinking, deciding, acting, and relating. These people are setting their minds on the things of the flesh. In other words, they are putting their attention on things like their own will, glory, and sufficiency. Now on the other hand, those who walk according to the Spirit, day by day, step by step, are looking to the resources and works of the Spirit of God. They set their minds on things of the Spirit. They set their minds on God's will and God's grace, which is our sufficiency.

Scripture confirms this:

> Those who are dominated by the sinful nature think about sinful things, but those who are controlled by the Holy Spirit think about things that please the Spirit. So letting your sinful nature control your mind leads to death. But letting the Spirit control your mind leads to life and peace. For the sinful nature is always hostile to God. It never did obey God's laws, and it never will. That's why those who are still under the control of their sinful nature can never please God. (Romans 8:5–8)

Real life begins when we are born again, receive the Holy Spirit, depend on the Holy Spirit, are led by the Holy Spirit, and then trust the Holy Spirit to direct our steps. In fact, remember Jesus' vital words to Nicodemus. Jesus replied, "I tell you the truth, unless you are born again you cannot see the Kingdom of God" (John 3:3).

Beware—Satan is trying to twist Christian truth and dilute the need to be born again. Moreover, Satan is attacking the person of Jesus, the holy, inspired Word of God, and works vehemently to deceive you in order to turn you to his deceptive way of seeing Christianity. Satan wants you to believe biblical truth is intolerant and to some degree the enemy. This is a lie straight from hell. Listen to God's heart. "For God loved the world so much that he gave his one and only Son, so that everyone who believes in him will not perish but have eternal life. God sent his Son into the world not to judge the world, but to save the world through him" (John 3:16–17). Why did He have to die? He came to free us from the curse and to conquer sin and death.

Sinner's Prayer

> God, my Father in heaven, You are holy and always do what is right. Thank You that You love me and have such compassion for me even though I have sinned against You. Thank You that You sent Jesus to destroy the curse of shame and guilt that separated me from Your unfailing love. Thank You that He died in my place. Please forgive me for my many sins and fill me with the Holy Spirit. I want to follow You, my living Savior. Thank You for accepting me as I am. I surrender to You this day and return my heart to You. In Jesus' name, amen.

Please understand we are saved or born again so that Jesus can impart His Holy Spirit into our hearts. Once we open our hearts, Jesus can by His Holy Spirit recreate us into His image. Having His divine power, we are enabled and gifted to share the gospel with those who are spiritually lost. We are saved to serve God, and during the tribulation God will use you powerfully to reveal His love. This book is a guide to help you quickly understand your calling and gifting. The following is a prophecy foretold by the prophet Isaiah, and it reveals the coming King Jesus in His first coming. He is coming again at the end of the tribulation and will rescue all who remain in Him. Draw near to Him and stand strong. He will never leave you or forsake you. He loves you profoundly and has forgiven you of all your sin. Believe! "All things are possible if you believe" (Mark 9:23).

Read Isaiah 53

Who has believed our message? To whom has the LORD revealed his powerful arm? My servant grew up in the LORD's presence like a tender green shoot, like a root in dry ground. There was nothing beautiful or majestic about his appearance, nothing to attract us to him. He was despised and rejected—a man of sorrows, acquainted with deepest grief. We turned our backs on him and looked the other way. He was despised, and we did not care. Yet it was our weaknesses he carried; it was our sorrows that weighed him down. And we thought his troubles were a punishment from God, a punishment for his own sins! But he was pierced for our rebellion, crushed for our sins. He was beaten so we could be whole. He was whipped so we could be healed. All of us, like sheep, have strayed away. We have left God's paths to follow our own. Yet the LORD laid on him the sins of us all. He was oppressed and treated harshly, yet he never said a word. He was led like a lamb to the slaughter. And as a sheep is silent before the shearers, he did not open his mouth. Unjustly condemned, he was led away. No one cared that he died without descendants, that his life was cut short in midstream but he was struck down for the rebellion of my people. He had done no wrong and had never deceived anyone. But he was buried like a criminal; he was put in a rich man's grave. But it was the LORD's good plan to crush him and cause him grief. Yet when his life is made an offering for sin, he will have many descendants. He will enjoy a long life, and the LORD's good plan will prosper in his hands. When he sees all that is accomplished by his anguish, he will be satisfied. And because of his experience, my righteous servant will make it possible for many to be counted righteous, for he will bear all their sins. I will give him the honors of a victorious soldier, because he exposed himself to death. He was counted among the rebels. He bore the sins of many and interceded for rebels. (Isaiah 53)

For this is how God loved the world: He gave his one and only Son, so that everyone who believes in him will not perish but have eternal life. (John 3:16)

CHAPTER 3

The Work of the Holy Spirit

But now I am (Jesus) going away to the one who sent me, and not one of you is asking where I am going. Instead, you grieve because of what I've told you. But in fact, it is best for you that I go away, because if I don't, the Advocate (Holy Spirit) won't come. If I do go away, then I will send him (The Holy Spirit) to you. *And when he comes, he will convict the world of its sin, and of God's righteousness, and of the coming judgment.* The world's sin is that it refuses to believe in me. Righteousness is available because I go to the Father, and you will see me no more. Judgment will come because the ruler of this world has already been judged. There is so much more I want to tell you, but you can't bear it now. When the Spirit of truth comes, *he will guide you into all truth. He will not speak on his own but will tell you what he has heard. He will tell you about the future.* He will bring me glory by telling you whatever he receives from me. All that belongs to the Father is mine; this is why I said, "The Spirit will tell you whatever he receives from me." John 16:5-15.

In all seriousness, what I believe the world needs most is the Holy Spirit, *which opens the heart to see true eternal reality.* To begin with, the Holy Spirit is working in the unseen realm to help you.

> The one who is the true light [Jesus], who gives light to everyone, was coming into the world. He came into the very world He created, but the world didn't recognize Him. He came to his own people, and even that none but God can satisfy a vacuum that only God they rejected him. But *to* *all who believed him and accepted him, he gave the right* *to become children of God. They are reborn—not with* *a physical birth resulting from human passion or plan,* *but a birth that comes from God.* So the Word [God] became human [Jesus] and made his home among us. He was full of unfailing love and faithfulness. And we have seen his glory, the glory of the Father's one and only Son. (John 1:9–14)

> There is no judgment against anyone who believes in him. *But anyone who does not believe in him has* *already been judged for not believing in God's one and* *only Son.* And the judgment is based on this fact: God's light came into the world, but people loved the darkness more than the light, for their actions were evil. All who do evil hate the light and refuse to go near it for fear their sins will be exposed. But those who do what is right come to the light so others can see that they are doing what God wants. (John 3:18–21)

If you have been chosen by God and you're pushing Him away, remember, if idolatry has blinded your eyes, God will take away all of the idols to reveal the truth that only an empty shell is left. Everyone is looking to worship something, and if it's not Jesus Christ, it will be an idol of some form or another. Turning to Christ means a complete commitment in which He becomes the center of your heart, passion, and worship.

What does the Holy Spirit do to help us? He guides us into all truth. To get started following Jesus, you need to get to know Him, and this happens as we read the Bible, pray, fellowship with other believers, trust Him, and obey Him. Practically speaking we all come just as we are, full of sin, bad habits, and idols. Through a process of setting us apart from our sin, the Holy Spirit and God's Word begin to renew our mind and set us free from sinful behaviors. The Scriptures declare that as we know Jesus better, His divine power will give us everything we need to live a godly life (2 Peter 1:3). If you're reading this, you are in most critical period of time. You maybe in the last seven years of the history of earth as we know it. You cannot afford to be careless about the destiny of your soul. Once you have surrendered completely to Christ as Lord, you must begin to trust Him and depend on Him completely to help you through the tribulation.

CHAPTER 4

How Can You Be Faithful?

1. *You must magnify the consequences of sin.*

   When you were slaves to sin, you were free from the obligation to do right. And what was the result? You are now ashamed of the things you used to do, things that end in eternal doom. But now you are free from the power of sin and have become slaves of God. Now you do those things that lead to holiness and result in eternal life. For the wages of sin is death, but the free gift of God is eternal life through Christ Jesus our Lord. (Romans 6:20–23)

   Don't you realize that you become the slave of whatever you choose to obey? You can be a slave to sin, which leads to death, or you can choose to obey God, which leads to righteous living. (Romans 6:16)

   An evil man is held captive by his own sins; they are ropes that catch and hold him. (Proverbs 5:22)

2. *You must make a commitment to God's standards*

   How can a young person stay pure? By obeying your word. (Psalm 119:9)

Run from anything that stimulates youthful lusts. Instead, pursue righteous living, faithfulness, love, and peace. Enjoy the companionship of those who call on the Lord with pure hearts. (2 Timothy 2:22)

3. *You must manage your mind.*

Don't copy the behavior and customs of this world, but let God transform you into a new person by changing the way you think. Then you will learn to know God's will for you, which is good and pleasing and perfect. (Romans 12:2)

And now, dear brothers and sisters, one final thing. Fix your thoughts on what is true, and honorable, and right, and pure, and lovely, and admirable. Think about things that are excellent and worthy of praise. (Philippians 4:8)

Temptation comes from our own desires, which entice us and drag us away. These desires give birth to sinful actions. And when sin is allowed to grow, it gives birth to death. So don't be misled, my dear brothers and sisters. Whatever is good and perfect comes down to us from God our Father, who created all the lights in the heavens. He never changes or casts a shifting shadow. He chose to give birth to us by giving us his true word. And we, out of all creation, became his prized possession. (James 1:14–18)

4. *You must maintain a constant vigil.*

You must be watchful to detect trouble and remain wakeful to be alert. Evil will increase and deception will be rampant. If you think you are standing strong, be careful not to fall. The temptations in your life are no different from what others experience. And God is faithful. He will not allow the temptation to be more than you can stand. When you are tempted, he will show you a way out so that you can endure. (1 Corinthians 10:12–13)

What If You Blow It?

- Recognize where you have gone wrong.
- Elect to change.
- Pray for forgiveness.
- Expect a battle.
- Negotiate a new course.
- Throw away the excuses.

But thank God! He gives us victory over sin and death through our Lord Jesus Christ. (1 Corinthians 15:57)

Always run to God and cry out to Jesus when you're convicted of sin. Don't try to hide in guilt or shame.

Simply trust Him and ask Him to deliver you from your sin. We are made right in God's sight when we trust in Jesus Christ to take away our sin. (Romans 3:22)

CHAPTER 5

The Power of Sharing Your Testimony

> And they have defeated him by the blood of the Lamb and by their testimony. And they did not love their lives so much that they were afraid to die. Therefore, rejoice, O heavens! And you who live in the heavens, rejoice! (Revelation 12:11–12)

Sharing your testimony is simply telling others how Jesus rescued you from your spiritual deception or blindness, namely sharing your story of how you were converted and born again. Conversion is often a unique process, and no two testimonies are the same. For each individual God initiates the process of salvation through conviction of the Holy Spirit. The Holy Spirit works to draw us to truth regarding our sin condition, our need for the righteousness of Christ Jesus, and the coming judgment for all who willfully suppress this revelation and invitation into God's kingdom.

During the dispensation of the church age, it may take several invitations through the Holy Spirit before we become willing to turn from our sin and the power of Satan and turn to Jesus to deny ourselves and take up our cross to follow Him. What does it mean to take up your cross and follow me? It means it's means following Jesus requires "dying to self." It's a call to absolute surrender. It means being willing to die in order to follow Jesus. Once grace has overshadowed our will and faith is birthed, we see our helpless, lost condition in ungodliness before a holy God, and we flee to Jesus for salvation. This is just a simple explanation of a very mysterious and complex process so please understand that the Bible says, "The wind blows wherever it wants. Just as you can hear the wind but can't tell where it comes from or where it is going, so you can't explain how people are born of the Spirit" (John 3:8). The most important point in sharing your testimony is to keep the focus on what knowing Jesus as Lord has done for you personally. The following is my testimony. Although it is rather complex, not all testimonies are. The greatest aspect of any testimony is that you once were blind and now you see the kingdom of God and its full reality.

To begin, let me share that I was thirty-seven years old before I was born again. My personal process of conversion was made up of difficult experiences that involved me developing a worldview that happiness in life was directly related to money, status, and prestige. I believed the message of the world's system, not the message of the gospel. This broad path is the path that the Bible says seems right to a man but ends in destruction.

As I grew up, my family seemed fine. We lived in a comfortable upper middle class neighborhood, had kind friends, and enjoyed all that life has to offer. My parents were very loving, and my father was a hard worker who provided us with all a child could desire materially. My mom had a belief in God, and we would attend Sunday school at times. Once when I was eleven we attended a Billy Graham crusade. This was the first time I heard the gospel of Jesus Christ. Billy's message was compelling as I considered the cross and the sacrifice Jesus made as my substitute. My brother and I went forward when Billy gave the invitation and said the sinner's prayer, along with hundreds of others. I assumed that we had believed and were ready to follow Jesus, yet our lives never really changed and neither did our desires. You might say our natural nature remained very self-centered, and we loved all the world had to offer.

Fast forward seven years and a crisis hit our family. My father decided to leave the family in pursuit of his personal dreams. My mom was left devastated with two sons who allowed hurt turn to anger and anger to rebellion. Our pristine life of wealth, security, and comfort had just collapsed, and all hell was breaking loose. Thank God my mom was born again and had help fighting through the agony of loss and anxiety that penetrated her heart to the very core.

After a year of very difficult suffering, my mom was able to slowly reenter society. I was struggling with the loss of my father's love and all he brought to our family. He was the sole provider and had provided an almost fairytale lifestyle. We lived on a private lake with fishing, swimming, boating, etc. The Rogue River ran alongside the lake and provided salmon and steelhead fishing, rafting, and swimming too. Moreover, we had access to twenty-five hundred acres for exploring, hunting, and four wheeling. To say the least, it seemed like paradise to fifteen- and sixteen-year-old boys.

Loss is painful and takes its toll, and we ended up losing the house and our relationship with my father and with my mother for a short time. Due to our rebellion my brother and I were asked to move into an apartment. During this season sin ran its course, and drugs, alcohol, women, and wild parties fulfilled our passions for lust. This wild ride ended when I was a passenger in a severe car accident that left me seriously injured, with an arm broken in several places and severely bruised ribs. This accident, although extremely devastating and painful, led me to move back in with my Christian mom. Soon after, my mom and I moved into a midsized home, and I returned to high school. My behavior remained controlled by my lust for pleasure and fun. You might say personal pleasure was the purpose of my life. I continued to find thrills in parties and worldly pleasure.

After high school I met a girl at a party, and she said she attended Apple Gate Christian fellowship, which just so happened to be the same church my mom attended. I decided I would give it a try, and upon hearing the teaching of the Word, I was moved to begin to seek this man called Jesus. As I drew near to God during my time there, I truly began to believe the gospel being taught. My behavior began to change. Even my words changed, and I enjoyed the teaching in fact so much so that I decided to be baptized. After the baptism I was sure I would be forever changed, yet upon my first major test, I failed. I had a level of belief, as many do after baptism, yet my religion lacked the power to save me. You see, I left the church to attend college, and very shortly after leaving, I returned very quickly to my old lifestyle of living for pleasure, self, and fun. I all but forgot about Jesus and His call to come out of the world system to know and love Him and others and instead dove head first into the broad path. I continued to practice and enjoy sin. My love for self and this world revealed that my profession of being a Christian was false. The Scriptures clearly reveal this fact:

> Those who have been born into God's family do not make a practice of sinning, because God's life is in them. So they can't keep on sinning, because they are children of God. So now we can tell who are children of God and who are children of the devil. Anyone who does not live righteously and does not love other believers does not belong to God. (1 John 3:9–10)

Moreover, many people may not be practicing the sin by breaking laws or even doing things our world defines as wrong, yet they remain in the practice of sin. The Scriptures declare in light of what Jesus has done for us, it is each of our moral duty to believe in Jesus and to do everything possible to help others to do the same. Many are guilty of the sin of doing nothing. Many choose the easy path of spiritual apathy or laziness. God's Word says, "Remember, it is sin to know what you ought to do and then not do it" (James 4:17). This definition below of love best defines evidence of the Holy Spirit's work in a genuine believer's heart.

Love is when you will do anything at your own expense to satisfy the needs of others, while lust is when you will do anything at the expense of others to satisfy your own needs. It is possible you were or may be left behind because you had a form of religion that lacked the genuine faith and love to truly believe. The tribulation is your last chance to turn from the power of Satan and your sin and deny yourself, take up your cross, and follow Jesus. Love's definition above best illustrates the spiritual reality of complete surrender. This would be a good time to ask yourself what have you truly lived for—to satisfy your own needs or the needs of others in gratitude for what Jesus has done for you on Calvary's cross? You can live as Christ lived, but you must be born again.

Proof of true conversion is seen by our actions, and my actions revealed I was truly motivated by lust, not love. I loved myself, pleasure, and money, and my life was clearly centered on pleasing myself, not on pleasing Jesus Christ, who died for me and through His sacrifice purchased me. You might say by claiming the right to live as I chose, I was robbing God of what was legally His through the death of His Son. Self-centered living at the expense of loving God and others is the path that seems right to many of us, yet it leads to death and eternal separation from God.

Living independently of God would prove to be a major catastrophe for me. First, I came down with extreme anxiety, and finding no relief, I entered into episodes of suicidal depression. The Scriptures say, "Anxiety in the heart of man causes depression"

(Proverbs 12:25). Keep in mind that in the spiritual definition, anxiety is simply another word for unbelief. One of the main symptoms of unbelief is fear. Fear can produce chemical changes in the body that lead to anxiety. So where does fear come from? If you drill down into the primitive root word for fear in the Strong's Hebrew Lexicon online, fear is called *guwr*, and this word means "To turn aside from the road." So my testimony serves as living proof that as I turned aside from the way (Jesus) to sin in the darkness of this world, fear and worry triggered anxiety, which ultimately triggered clinical depression.

That being said, listen carefully. The extreme suffering served a very valuable purpose in setting me free from self-deception. It served as a check engine light on the dashboard of my life as I was driving 180 degrees in the wrong direction, without any fear of God and the judgment forthcoming on all who reject Him.

To make a long story short, I am just going to say that over five years I suffered with periods of extreme suicidal depression. I saw several doctors, counselors, psychiatrists, and psychologists. I took over thirty different medications; I was hospitalized on four different occasions in mental hospitals. I believe the origin of my illness was stress, so I believed if I could apply all the world's remedies to deal with stress, I could beat this horrible disease. Unfortunately, I refused to believe that God could help me or even would after all the sin I had racked up, so I worked only on the horizontal realm of the material world, looking desperately to save my life. I changed careers, diet, exercise programs, and living expenses. I even went so far as to close my business and move my family into our mother-in-law's house. I was trying to eliminate all stress to see if I might survive, but unfortunately even receiving financial support from the state's disability program would not solve my problem, and after years of fighting, I grew weary and began to plan my suicide.

One morning I drove out to a mountain lake and stopped my car at the shore of a park called Seattle Bar. In a state of terror and unrelenting fear, I took a razor blade and cut my wrist. Prior to this I had drank several beers and taken a handful of anxiety relief medication. I passed out, certain I was entering death's door, when suddenly a cool breeze woke me. Looking down at my wrist, I was surprised to see blood but not enough to kill me. In a state of confusion at the realization of my failed attempt, I got up and staggered to the car. I had a backup plan, and I had a hose and duct tape standing by. After I taped the hose to the exhaust pipe, I pulled the hose up to the window, and it was three inches short of reaching inside.

Frustrated and in pain as my wrist was deeply cut and stinging, I climbed in the car. I began driving up the curvy road and thought through the idea of driving off a cliff. Before I had a chance, I accidently drove off a very steep embankment. Before I began to roll down the hundred-foot embankment, I suddenly hit a grove of trees. My vehicle flipped up on its side as I impacted the trees and fell back to the ground. I was shaken up but certainly not dead. My vehicle was totaled, and now I was faced with my greatest fear. I had to crawl up the bank on my hands and knees to get to the road to try to find help.

I found help and was once again taken to the hospital for stitches and a weeklong stay in the mental ward called 2N. They had no other rooms, so they put me in the lockup room with padded walls. This only served to add terror to my already overwhelmed psyche. For three days I laid on a small mattress covered with a white sheet. I suffered at levels internally emotionally that I did not know existed until then. No words could describe the horror of such deep depression and unrelenting anxiety.

I was thirty-four years old at this point. I had a wife who was still hanging in there and three precious children. To say the least, we were all losing hope rather quickly. I believed I was damaged goods and that my family did not deserve me and my heavy burden, so while I was in the hospital, I planned another suicide attempt. I worked hard to get out so I could end it once and for all.

After I was released, I went to a local store and bought a shotgun and a box of shells. Next I proceeded a nearby mountain and stopped the car near the top. It seemed like the perfect day to die. I knew I had given it my best effort, and I was convinced I would be placed in a long-term mental hospital eventually anyway. So I loaded the gun and fired a shot to make certain it worked. Then I turned the barrel on myself and inserted it into my mouth. I would not fail at suicide twice!

As I prepared to execute myself, thoughts began to flood my mind. First, the thoughts were, *Do it. You have tried everything.*

There is no hope. No good God would let you suffer like this. Pull the trigger and the suffering ends. But after those thoughts passed, I heard a still, small voice in my heart that said, *Do you know where you're going?* Then I remember thinking, *What if there is a hell, and what if my suffering is only going to get worse? I'll be all alone, with no family, in the darkest dark.* I began to tremble at the thought of such hopeless, unending terror. I dropped the gun and stepped back. At that moment I knew I could not commit suicide. I determined, *Even if I never feel better than now, I will die of natural causes.* That moment of stark reality facing the gate of hell was way too costly to take a risk with. So I left the mountain with a new fear of the Lord and a strong conviction that I was not a born-again Christian.

It took one year of recovery before I entered the work force again and began a new life. After working as a national sales trainer for a year, the most amazing blessing came my way. Please keep in mind I was not a Christian and I was not interested in being one at this point. That being said, on a Sunday night in September 1999, the vice president of one of the nation's most premier swim spa and hot tub manufacturers contacted me. I could hardly believe the conversation and the offer they made me to join them as a business development consultant.

The manufacturer was located in San Diego California, and I was offered a territory that included California, Nevada, and Hawaii. The most amazing part of the offer was the extremely generous commission. The region was nearing 5 million in sales, and I was to receive 4.5 percent. I wasn't sure I was ready for such a major position, but I decided to take it, and the rest is history. I worked for them from 1999 till 2008. But something life changing happened during my first two years of work there. Since I still lived in Oregon, I drove every other week into California. My mom, always seeking to help me find a relationship with Jesus, gave me a box of tapes and CDs that contained sermons from a local pastor. For some reason I began listening to sermons as I drove, and the more I heard, the more I was drawn into the story of the gospel.

I decided to attend church on Sundays with my family and began to grow in the knowledge of Jesus as I continued to seek Him. If only I had obeyed the Bible and not just listened to the pastors, I may have turned to God much sooner. The Bible says, "And this is the way to have eternal life—to know you, the only true God, and Jesus Christ, the one you sent to earth" (John 17:3). Moreover, the Scriptures declare,

> The law of the LORD *is* perfect, converting the soul; The testimony of the LORD *is* sure, making wise the simple; The statutes of the LORD *are* right, rejoicing the heart; The commandment of the LORD *is* pure, enlightening the eyes; The fear of the LORD *is* clean, enduring forever; The judgments of the LORD *are* true *and* righteous altogether. More to be desired *are they* than gold, Yea, than much fine gold; Sweeter also than honey and the honeycomb. Moreover by them Your servant is warned, *And* in keeping them *there is* great reward. (Psalm 19:7–11)

After seeking the Lord through sermons and His Word for about a year, I was converted or what Scripture calls born again. It was Easter Sunday on April 15, 2001, when I audibly declared Jesus to be Lord. At that moment something very life changing happened as I experienced a peace that surpassed understanding and the veil was lifted from my eyes. It was on that day that the Holy Spirit was imparted into my heart, and I would never be the same.

Once I was able to see the truth regarding the reality between the material world and the spiritual, I was able to look at the cross of Calvary with completely new understanding. This new view of Christ's work on the cross brought a radical sense of godly sorrow over my sins and a newfound sense of deep gratitude and respect for the incalculably high cost Jesus was willing to pay to save an unworthy sinner like me. Frankly, for the past thirty-eight years I had been His enemy and was actually working against His universal plan of salvation, not unlike many of you, due to unbelief and ignorance. At this revelation my desires radically changed, and I was no longer the same person. I had a deep desire to know all I could about Jesus, and reading the Bible became a passion. I had a strong desire to join Him in His work of salvation.

Within three months I was sharing my testimony and the gospel at several churches, church camps, and funerals, at a Bible training center in Haiti, on radio programs, in Israel, at mental hospitals, and at recovery centers. Over the next eight years, from 2001 to 2008, I literally chose to live as Jesus lived, and I helped homeless people, drug addicts, sex addicts, homosexuals, men addicted to pornography, the mentally ill, suffers of anorexia, those trapped in false religions, etc. I trusted Christ to use the gift He gave me, and He led me from one divine appointment to another day by day as I remained teachable and open to taking risks for His name's sake. During this life-changing experience, I continued to run my own business as a development consultant representing a major manufacturer. In addition, I went to a two-year Bible school for three hours each week to grow in knowledge of God's grace and love.

Please listen carefully to my testimony. All Christians will share in both Christ's glory and suffering. If you fail to stand strong and continue to depend completely on Jesus for strength and hope, the Scripture declares,

> Stay alert! Watch out for your great enemy, the devil. He prowls around like a roaring lion, looking for someone to devour. Stand firm against him, and be strong in your faith. Remember that your Christian brothers and sisters all over the world are going through the same kind of suffering you are. (1 Peter 5:8–9)

The sin of being careless about experiencing a genuine relationship with Jesus rooted in knowing Him intimately will steal the very things you value the most as Satan is given access to devour your closest relationships. I am a witness that your sin and the sin of others in your life will bring extremely painful suffering and deception. Yet God is a Creator and His will is to draw near to you, if you are willing to seek Him with all your heart. He will recreate you even though you have been completely destroyed by the heavy weight of sin's consequences. Please don't give up hope, don't rely on your own understanding, and work hard at growing in faith, and God will deliver you from the tribulation.

> In his kindness God called you to share in his eternal glory by means of Christ Jesus. So after you have suffered a little while, he will restore, support, and strengthen you, and he will place you on a firm foundation. All power to him forever! Amen. (1 Peter 5:10–11)

I really want to make a strong point here regarding abiding in Christ. To abide is to dwell with or to remain very close to. Moreover, preparation is very important because none of us know what tests, trials, or tribulations are ahead. I am so thankful that I loved God and invested in His kingdom with my very best effort, because when my marriage was destroyed, that was only one facet of a rugged series of test I faced simultaneously, severe enough to destroy any man. The only way I survived from 2008 to 2014 was by the strength God provided, the prayers of faithful family and friends, and the support of an extremely loving mother.

From 2001 through 2008, I was a successful businessman and evangelist serving Christ Jesus. In 2008 I recall kneeling in my office and praying. I surrendered everything I had, including myself, to God and His will. I wanted to know Him better. I wanted to see my marriage healed, and I wanted to fulfill my calling, which I believed involved raising my six precious children in Christ and serving in fulltime ministry. If I had it my way, I was going to be promoted by Jesus into a great evangelistic calling, like Billy Graham. My marriage would be healed and my children spared the horrors of divorce. What happened next exceeded my worst fears. Days after the prayer, I lost my contract and a very high-paying job. Next every attempt to launch a ministry failed. Looking back to the work force, I attempted several careers, only to fail, one after another. Finally the pressure mounted, and I feel into a deep depression. My children had to be removed from their private Christian school, my marriage was spiraling out of control, and for the first time, my faith began to waver.

I could not believe God would allow this to happen after I had served Him faithfully for eight years. Under tremendous stress and fear, I headed for the bar and returned to drinking beer to ease my pain. This only complicated the problems and left me in a deeper state of discouragement. By this time my financial empire had collapsed, and I was facing bankruptcy and a foreclosure on my family's home. I drove a Lincoln Navigator, and I had to sell it, as well as my custom billiard room and deluxe spa. Basically I was caught dead center in the middle of my own personal tribulation. As the fear and stress of losing it all weighed heavily on my heart, I believed I was heading back into suicidal depression, which I thought would start the whole nightmare of unyielding suffering over again once again facing such tremendous loss, yet my faith had been growing for eight years and just as God's word promised, "By His divine power, God has given us everything we need for living a godly life. We have received all of this by coming to know him, the one who called us to himself by means of his marvelous glory and excellence." 2 Peter 1:3. I was being empowered by God to endure the tribulation that would only continue to increase in loss, suffering, and intensity. This testimony is told to reveal that God through divine power has given you all you need no matter how dark and hopeless your circumstances get. Stand strong and remain in Christ by faith. Your faith will grow and God will deliver each of you in His perfect timing. As you read this testimony, you will see that my suffering has a purpose and this book is that purpose so that you will see God save me from what would appear to be against all odds.

The Savior of Israel is our Savior today ... Jesus is the same yesterday, today, and forever.

> But now, O Jacob, listen to the LORD who created you. For I am the LORD, your God, O Israel, the one who formed you says, "Do not be afraid, for I have ransomed you. I have called you by name; you are mine. When you go through deep waters, I will be with you. When you go through rivers of difficulty, you will not drown. When you walk through the fire of oppression, you will not be burned up; the flames will not

consume you. The Holy One of Israel, your
Savior. (Isaiah 43:1–3)

One thing I did every day was worship the Lord by singing
in my car along with my favorite CDs. Moreover, I leaned on
Christian brothers and sisters for support, encouragement, and
prayer. As I mentioned, God's grace is sufficient, and it comes in
many forms—music, the Word, friends, family, God's creation,
the church, etc. It is imperative that you huddle up with other
Christians in tribulation. We are created for relationship, and
you'll have a very difficult time trying to make it alone. Please
let my testimony reveal through a true modern example that
God is with you no matter how dark and painful circumstances
get. He will never leave you, so please don't leave Him. God
promises:

> The LORD is close to the brokenhearted; he
> rescues those whose spirits are crushed. The
> righteous person faces many troubles, but the
> LORD comes to the rescue each time. (Psalm
> 34:18–19)

Before I conclude this testimony, let me say again, knowing
Jesus personally is the key to survival and ultimately eternal life.
In 2 Peter 1:3 the Scriptures declare, "As we know Jesus better
His divine power gives us everything we need to live a godly
life." The divine power is Christ's Spirit living in you. I had
many years to prepare for this personal tribulation, yet many

of you may be newly converted. Please simply trust in Christ Jesus. He will do in you and through you infinitely more than you would ever dream. The most vital issue is that you remain in Him. God has given you the armor of God, and you must put it on daily. I have provided a prayer for applying the armor of God in the chapter on prayer. Moreover, meditate on the Word day and night. This has been an essential part of growing in knowledge, wisdom, and grace for me. We can defeat Satan, for the Scriptures declare:

> Dear friends, do not believe everyone who claims to speak by the Spirit. You must test them to see if the spirit they have comes from God. For there are many false prophets in the world. This is how we know if they have the Spirit of God: If a person claiming to be a prophet acknowledges that Jesus Christ came in a real body, that person has the Spirit of God. But if someone claims to be a prophet and does not acknowledge the truth about Jesus, that person is not from God. Such a person has the spirit of the Antichrist, which you heard is coming into the world and indeed is already here.
>
> But you belong to God, my dear children. You have already won a victory over those people, because the Spirit who lives in you is greater than the spirit who lives in the world. Those people belong to this world, so they speak from the world's viewpoint, and the world listens to them. But we belong to God, and those who know God listen to us. If they do not belong to God, they do not listen to us. That is how we know if someone

has the Spirit of truth or the spirit of deception. 1 John:1-6.

Please pray and ask God to breathe the power of His Holy Spirit into your hearts as you experience the gospel. The Scriptures declare this:

> Then Jesus explained: "My nourishment comes from doing the will of God, who sent me, and from finishing his work. You know the saying, 'Four months between planting and harvest.' But I say, wake up and look around. The fields are already ripe for harvest. The harvesters are paid good wages, and the fruit they harvest is people brought to eternal life. What joy awaits both the planter and the harvester alike! You know the saying, 'One plants and another harvests.' And it's true. I sent you to harvest where you didn't plant; others had already done the work, and now you will get to gather the harvest." (John 4:34–38)

I have learned the best path is to follow Jesus. Jesus had a purpose, and that was to make His Father real to an unbelieving world. As we get to know Him, He will provide us with everything we need to share the gospel with a lost and dying world. If you want to stay healthy spiritually, ask the Father, "What can I do to help the family? What can I do to help the lost?" He will answer your prayers as He has mine, and even if the cup spills, through your brokenness He will pour out blessings on others far greater than you would imagine. Take a risk for Jesus, lay down your life for a friend, and count it all joy because your name is written in the Book of Life.

After all of this tribulation and subsequent confusion and suffering, I have learned that suffering has a very important purpose in the life of true believers. Suffering destroys pride and grows faith. Purifies us from unrighteousness, increases our capacity for joy and enables us to march in the dark on the narrow path with infallible accuracy by God's grace.

In closing, I never took my eyes off the one who so graciously rescued me from this world, and as a result I learned some valuable lessons from my tribulation.

1. God is love. The key to my survival was to continue to love God and His children in tribulation.
2. There is fun in sin for a season.
3. You will reap what you sow later than you sow and more than you sow.
4. Obedience leads to blessings, and obedient people suffer.
5. The Christian life requires a complete commitment.
6. Life without Christ is meaningless.
7. Expectations will end differently than we dreamed.
8. Loss of loved ones is extremely painful, yet God's grace is sufficient to heal.
9. Money will never bring lasting peace or contentment.
10. Materialism can be a great distraction.
11. Bad things happen to good people.

12. All suffering has a purpose, and many blessing are folded inside to be released at the perfect time.

13. Life is not fair, and neither was the cross.

14. We all owe Christ a debt we can never repay.

15. Following Christ may cost you everything you possess, but it is well worth it.

16. Nothing compares to knowing the love of Christ Jesus.

17. Heaven is real, and so is hell.

18. Everyone who wants to be saved will be.

19. Satan is real and waits for the perfect time to destroy you. Abide in Jesus; Satan can't touch Him.

20. There are only two Fathers, Satan and God. You are either submitted to one or the other. Love God with all your heart, mind, soul, and strength.

CHAPTER 6

What Do We Pray?

Fifty-Seven Words That Changed the World

The Lord's Prayer

> Pray like this: Our Father in heaven, may your name be kept holy. May your Kingdom come soon. May your will be done on earth, as it is in heaven. Give us today the food we need, and forgive us our sins, as we have forgiven those who sin against us. And don't let us yield to temptation, but rescue us from the evil one. (Matthew 6:9–13)

"If you forgive those who sin against you, your heavenly Father will forgive you. But if you refuse to forgive others, your Father will not forgive your sins" (Matthew 6:14–15). It is very important that you seek our Lord and forgiveness for any offenses, grudges, or hurt you may be holding against another. Look to the cross to discover that none of us have the right to hold onto a grudge or seek revenge. Jesus has paid in full for all sin. That includes the sins of others who have betrayed or hurt us badly. We all have been saved by grace and owe Jesus a debt we could never repay, so let go of that grudge and leave the issue at the cross, where the blood of Jesus covers all sin.

A Practical Prayer

First, every morning I encourage you to talk to the Lord. The Bible says:

> Don't worry about anything; instead, pray about everything. Tell God what you need, and thank him for all he has done. Then you will experience God's peace, which exceeds anything we can understand. His peace will guard your hearts and minds as you live in Christ Jesus. (Philippians 4:5–6)

I encourage you to pray about everything. You are in the tribulation, and you will need to pray continually, drawing upon the divine power and comfort of our Lord.

One of the best habits you can develop is putting on *the armor of God* every morning. God has provided all you need to live a godly life even in crisis, yet you must put on the armor and prepare daily.

Each morning say something like this:

> Good morning, Lord. Thank You for assuring me of victory today. By faith I choose to follow Your battle plan and to prepare myself according to Your instructions. To prepare myself for the battle ahead, by faith I will be honest. Renew my mind to what is true. Fill me with the truth.

Expose in my heart the lies that I am tempted to believe. The truth is that You are the Sovereign God who loves me and cares for me. The truth about me is that I am Your child—bought and paid for. Nothing can separate me from Your love. By faith I put on the breastplate of righteousness. Today I am committed to doing what is right. I pray that I would be known as one who does what is right regardless of what it costs me. Allow the righteousness of Christ to shine through me today.

I now take up the shield of faith. My faith is in You and You alone. Apart from You, I can do nothing. In You, I can do all things. Everything that comes against me must come through You, for I am in You. As You walked without sin on this earth, live without sin through me today. By faith I claim victory over _____ (list some of the temptations you know you will face that day—pride, laziness, drug abuse, alcohol abuse, materialism, greed, lying, sexual immorality, violence, family disunity, etc., just to name a few. You personally fill in the blank with whatever you struggle with.) When I face these temptations, remind me that the victory has already been won.

By faith I put on the helmet of salvation. Thank You for saving me. Thank You for forgiving me. Thank You for sending the Holy Spirit to live inside me. Holy Spirit, I surrender my will to You today. I surrender my thoughts to You. I choose to take every thought captive to the obedience of Christ. And last, I take up the sword of the Spirit, which is the Word of God. (Then

claim several specific promises from Scripture.
See God's promises listed in this book. So Lord,
I now go rejoicing that You have chosen me to
represent You to this lost world. May others see
Jesus in me. May Satan and his hosts shudder as
Your power is manifest through me. In Jesus'
name I pray. Amen.

This is an excellent prayer to pray each morning before you
start your day. You will need a daily covering during tribulation.
Pray this with your family.

Why Pray? Because Scripture Reveals Its Power!

And all things you ask in *prayer*, believing, you
will receive … for one another so that you may
be healed. (Matthew 7:7–8)

God said to the prophet Isaiah, "Come now, and
let us reason together." Are any of you suffering
hardships? You should pray. Are any of you
happy? You should sing praises. Are any of you
sick? You should call for the elders of the church
to come and pray over you, anointing you with
oil in the name of the Lord. Such a prayer offered
in faith will heal the sick, and the Lord will make
you well. And if you have committed any sins,
you will be forgiven. Confess your sins to each
other and pray for each other so that you may be
healed. The earnest prayer of a righteous person
has great power and produces wonderful results.
Elijah was as human as we are, and yet when he
prayed earnestly that no rain would fall, none fell
for three and a half years! Then, when he prayed

again, the sky sent down rain and the earth began
to yield its crops. (James 5:14–18)

Each of us has prayed about situations and for other people
without seeing results. When that happens, it's easy to become
discouraged. Rather than give up, we should review our lives to
see if we need to alter something.

Practical Prayers to Pray for Non-Christians

- that God will draw them to Himself
- that they would seek to know God
- that they would believe Scripture
- that Satan would bound from blinding them to truth
- that the Holy Spirit would work in them
- that God would send someone to lead them to Christ
- that they would believe in Christ as Savior
- that they would turn from sin
- that they would confess Christ as Lord
- that they would yield all to follow Christ

Be confident: "Confess your sins to each other and pray for each
other so that you may be healed. The earnest prayer of a righteous
person has great power and produces wonderful results. James
5:16." *God is listening, friend. Trust Him.*

Ask God to Do the Following for Non-Christians

- send the Holy Spirit to convict them of sin, righteousness, and coming judgment
- provide the gift of humility, repentance, faith, obedience, and complete surrender
- bind all of Satan's and his emissaries' strategies
- bind all authority that your loved ones have given to Satan
- weaken and demolish every dominion, authority, power of darkness, and wicked spirit in the heavenly realm who have strategized to hinder salvation
- assign holy angels to engage in direct combat against all strongholds of evil
- reveal the true condition of the unbeliever's heart and provide revelation of the love found at the cross

How to Pray for Other Christians

- Thank God for their faith and changed lives.
- Ask God to help them know what He wants them to do (His will).
- Ask God to give them deep spiritual understanding and wisdom.
- Ask the Holy Spirit to reveal the depths of the Father's love for them.
- Ask God to help them focus on knowing Him personally.

- Ask God for divine power so they may live godly lives.
- Ask God to give them strength, power, endurance, and love.
- Ask God to give them in joy and thankfulness.
- Ask God to keep them from temptation and evil.

Pray all of the above for the *one hundred forty-four thousand witnesses and the two witnesses.* Pray with other brothers and sisters as often as you can. Remember, we are a family, each member being unique, and by sticking together we gain strength. Don't try to make it alone.

Spiritual Warfare

Let me introduce you to the reality of Satan. Satan is a deceiver; he targets your mind, and uses the weapon of lies. He tries to get you to doubt God's word. Satan's purpose is to make you ignorant of God's will, your defense the Inspired Word of God. We must know God's word, we must pray God's word, and we must memorize and obey God's word. We must use God's word. Pray this prayer and look to it as an example of how to fight Satan.

Spiritual Warfare Prayer

Today I claim for _____, the full victory the Lord Jesus Christ has won over Satan and all his demons. I am thankful, heavenly Father, that the weapons of our warfare are not carnal but mighty through You to the pulling down of strongholds, to the casting down of imaginations and every high thing that exalts itself against the knowledge of God.

In the name of the Lord Jesus Christ, I ask You to bring all the power of the incarnation, resurrection, ascension, and glorification of my Lord Jesus Christ directly against all spirits and demons of darkness seeking to destroy_____ and against anything that would stand itself against the knowledge of God in _____'s life.

In the name of the Lord Jesus Christ, I take back any ground _____ may have given Satan, and I ask You to break any satanic and demonic links or ties in _____'s life.

In the name of the Lord Jesus Christ, I stand in the gap for _____. I submit myself to

God and resist the Devil and ask You to command him to flee from_____. Loose the Holy Spirit to bind up all of _____'s wounds and fill the void by ministering to him or her love, peace, joy, and all the other fruits of the spirit in such abundance that there will be no room for any evil to find lodging. _____ is bought with the blood of the Lord Jesus Christ, and his or her life will bring Him glory.

I pray that the eyes of _____'s heart will be enlightened so he or she may know the hope to which You have called him or her. Lord, release the riches of Your glorious divine power and inheritance in the saints for _____, who shall believe. I pray that _____'s love abounds more and more in the knowledge of the Father's love from him or her. Help him or her to look to You for help for acquiring wisdom and knowledge so he or she will be able to discern what is best and may be pure and blameless until the day of Christ Jesus, filled with the fruits of righteousness that come through the Lord.

I pray that _____, being rooted and established in love, may have power together with all the saints to grasp how wide and long and high and deep is the love of Christ.

Father, wash him or her in the water of the Word, and impute Your Holy Spirit into his or her heart. Wash him or her in the blood of the Lamb that was slain for his or her personal sins. Cleanse him or her from all unrighteousness. Father, refine him or her, and set him or her free from the poison of pride. Dispel his or her pride and replace it with grace and Your Holy Spirit so _____ may know and walk to the full measure of all the fullness of You, God.

Comfort him or her when he or she suffers and strengthen him or her through each trial and test he or she must face. May he or she always remember that You are always with him or her no matter how severe the suffering may become, and remind him or her that You suffer with him or her and that You have overcome the world and You will never leave of forsake him or her. Give him or her courage and bravery to persist until the end.

I am confident of this—that You, Father, who began a good work in_____ will carry it on to completion until the day of Christ Jesus, so I lift him or her up to you in Jesus' holy name. Amen. By Katie Kee, Sipirtual Training, Medford, Oregon. Xulon Press. 1999.

> Loving heavenly Father, I come in humble obedience to use the weapons of my warfare against the darkness that is seeking to rule the people of our city, country, and world. I affirm that the weapons You have given me have divine power that is sufficient to demolish every stronghold Satan has to hold back Your plan.
>
> In the Lord's Jesus Christ's mighty name, I use the weapons of my warfare to weaken and demolish every dominion, authority, power of darkness, and wicked spirit in the heavenly realm who has strategized to hinder revival. In the name of the Lord Jesus Christ and by the power of His blood, Father, pull down all levels of the strongholds of _____.

1. Pornography
2. Slothfulness and carelessness with the Word
3. Prayerlessness

4. Unbelief

5. Willful suppression of the truth

6. Self-love and greed

7. Materialism

8. Pride and spiritual indifference

9. Alcohol and drug addiction

10. Sexual immorality

11. Religious cults: Mormonism, Jehovah's Witnesses, Islam, Buddhism, Hinduism, new age beliefs

12. Antichrist delusions

13. Abortion

14. Homosexuality

15. Satan worship

This is only a suggested list that is not exhaustive; please pray for the pulling down of all satanic, fleshly, and world system strongholds. If idolatry has blinded one's eyes, God will take away all of the idols to reveal the truth that only an empty shell is left. This is one of the purposes of the tribulation.

Following is my personal prayer in my personal tribulation, written on September 11, 2013.

Dear Father,

Thank You for the cross and Your grace, mercy, and forgiveness. Apart from You I can do nothing good. Thank You for choosing to live Your sinless life in me. Lord, how deeply I have grown to hate sin and its miserable consequences, yet I praise You for Your promise that You will work all things together for good for those who love You and are called according to Your purpose. Denying self and taking up my cross has proved to be difficult, even as You said it would be. Thank You for comforting me and strengthening me. You are holding me with Your righteous right hand, and I am safe and secure in Your everlasting grip. Thank You for being faithful to love me by preparing me, enabling me, and sustaining me through tribulation that leaves me broken, without understanding.

Following You has cost me almost everything I once treasured and even loved. That's not to say that all is permanently lost, yet in the depth of my current darkness, it feels so painful and hopeless. The hardest of all consequences of my sin has been the loss of my wife and to a large degree the loss of any love relationship with my older children. Although You have allowed much suffering, You have also provided sufficient grace, truth, and love. It is by Your grace and divine power that I have endured losing my home, my career, my family, and nearly all my material possessions. The faith that is called for under such brokenness and confusion can only come from Your unconditional love.

Thank You, Father, for Jesus and the Holy Spirit, who are leading me home to You. The key to surviving in tribulation can be found only in drawing near to You and allowing the light of Your reality and presence to extinguish the darkness of our hearts. Please provide me with Your wisdom and Your understanding of the depths of Your love for me despite my current circumstances. Teach me to walk with You daily, to depend on You completely, to trust in You in spite of my fear. Dispel my pride, and fill me with Your Holy Spirit and grace. Help me to help others and to serve even in the face of discouragement and unbelief. Help me, dear Lord, with my unbelief, and help me believe that every promise in Your Word is true. In Jesus' name, amen.

CHAPTER 7

The Most Important Goal Now Is to Grow to Know Jesus Better

The apostle Peter gives us excellent instructions on how to do this. As we know Jesus better, His divine power gives us everything we need for living a godly life.

> In light of the fact that we have everything we need to endure and live a godly life; in light of the fact that have been given hundreds of promises so graciously; in light of the fact that we are free from the grasp of lust, we are to be those who add to their faith diligently.(2 Peter 1:3)

We grow to know Jesus better through studying His Word with a motive of getting to know Him personally and intimately. We must learn what He likes and dislikes. This will help us obey.

> By his divine power, God has given us everything we need for living a godly life. We have received all of this by coming to know him, the one who called us to himself by means of his marvelous glory and excellence. And because of his glory and excellence, he has given us great and precious promises. These are the promises that enable you to share his divine nature and escape the world's corruption caused by human desires. In

view of all this, make every effort to respond to God's promises. Supplement your faith with a generous provision of moral excellence, and moral excellence with knowledge, and knowledge with self-control, and self-control with patient endurance, and patient endurance with godliness, and godliness with brotherly affection, and brotherly affection with love for everyone. (2 Peter 1:3–7)

Let's drill down into this passage to gain further insight on getting to know God personally.

1. *Go for Virtue and Moral Excellence*

How? Avoid the darkness of this culture portrayed

- on the screen;
- in song lyrics; and
- in questionable jokes and foul language.

Let the customs of this world system have no place in your lives.

2. *Add to Virtue Knowledge*

Avoid filling your spirit with conversations about the world, gossip, criticism, negativism, complaining, and the like. From the abundance of your heart your mouth speaks, so listen carefully to your words and let God transform your heart and words by the renewing of your mind. This renewing takes place as we avoid the world's culture and junk and replace it with healthy time spent in God's Word. If you're all filled up with the stuff of the world, you will have no appetite for God's Word. Ultimately, you will not be able to extract knowledge, so carve out some time every day to search for knowledge in the Scriptures.

3. *Add to Knowledge Self-Control*

As you are being renewed by the divine power of God through His Word, you will begin to grow in self-control. What is self-control from God's perspective? To understand, let's look at another word called *meekness*. What is meekness? calm temper of mind, not easily provoked (James 3:13). The idea of biblical self-control can best be seen in Jesus. Suffering is part of the Christian life, and in this season it may be more intense than ever. Yet you must remain faithful by believing that our heavenly Father loves us with a love we can never doubt. Ultimately nothing but good can ever come from Him to us. Whatever the form the painful events may be, we know it enfolds a blessing.

> "We should look on the inevitable, not as a decree of stern fate to which we can only submit, but as a revealing of the Fathers will, and therefore something holy and sacred, something, too in which a thousand blessings of love are folded up.
> —J. R. Miller, The Master's Blesseds. Swengel, Pennsylvania. Reiner Publication. 1977, pg35

4. *Add to Self-Control Patience*

If we're not careful, we can become impatient with those who are not believers. In his book J.R. Miller tells the story of two birds that are both captive in a wire cage. The first bird flies violently against the wires of its cage, trying to escape, but it only beats and bruises its own breast and wings. The wiser bird finds itself shut in the cage, unable to escape, and begins to sing, filling its prison with sweet music, and it spares itself all hurt. It shows a spirit of patience and trust. J. R. Miller tells a story in his book *The Master's Blesseds*. Swengel, Pennsylvania. Reiner Publication. 1977, pg 35. This is a good time to point out that I have placed many beautiful worship songs in this book for you.

5. *Add Patience to Godliness*

It is important for us to let the Holy Spirit work through us to defend righteousness.

6. *Add to Godliness Brotherly Kindness*

Brotherly kindness keeps godliness from becoming harsh. Nothing hurts one's life as resentment does. The damage our words do cannot be taken back, so be very slow to speak and quick to listen. No one cares how much you know until they know how much you care. Let the Spirit lead you compassionately on this journey.

7. *Add to Brotherly Affection—Love*

Agape love is love for the sake of loving, expecting nothing in return. The degree to which you add these qualities to your life will be the degree to which you will be fruitful and productive in your knowledge of the Lord.

> The more you grow like this, the more productive
> and useful you will be in your knowledge of our
> Lord Jesus Christ. (2 Peter 1:8)

We all can bring glory to God when we do what we were created to do. God has provided all we need; we must add it unto our hearts through knowing Him intimately.

> And this is the way to have eternal life—to know
> you, the only true God, and Jesus Christ, the one
> you sent to earth. (John 17:3)

Your love and knowledge for God will be in direct parallel to your love and knowledge of His Word. Let me share a little song: "If you don't read your Bible and you don't pray every day, you will shrink, shrink, shrink, but if you do read your Bible and you do pray every day, you will grow, grow, grow!" We should read the Bible because we want to know Him better so we can love Him and others more.

CHAPTER 8

Beware of False Prophets and Teachers

In the tribulation period, there will be many false prophets who come on the scene. Spirituality will become very deceptive and confusing. Remember, you have the Holy Spirit and God's Word to direct your steps, so depend fully on Him and trust no man.

It is better to take refuge in the LORD, than to trust in people. (Psalm 118:8)

> These people are false apostles. They are deceitful workers who disguise themselves as apostles of Christ. But I am not surprised! *Even Satan disguises himself as an angel of light.* So it is no wonder that his servants also disguise themselves as servants of righteousness. In the end they will get the punishment their wicked deeds deserve. (2 Corinthians 11:13–15)

Please be very careful who you trust. Rely on the Holy Spirit to provide discernment as it relates to who is safe or not. Many will claim to be believers of Christ yet will be wolves in sheep's clothing. The Bible warns about these people in Jude 1:

> In the same way, these people—who claim authority from their dreams—live immoral lives, defy

authority, and scoff at supernatural beings. But even Michael, one of the mightiest of the angels did not dare accuse the devil of blasphemy, but simply said, "The Lord rebuke you!" (This took place when Michael was arguing with the devil about Moses' body.) But these people scoff at things they do not understand. Like unthinking animals, they do whatever their instincts tell them, and so they bring about their own destruction. What sorrow awaits them! For they follow in the footsteps of Cain, who killed his brother. Like Balaam, they deceive people for money. And like Korah, they perish in their rebellion. When these people eat with you in your fellowship meals commemorating the Lord's love, they are like dangerous reefs that can shipwreck you. They are like shameless shepherds who care only for themselves. They are like clouds blowing over the land without giving any rain. They are like trees in autumn that are doubly dead, for they bear no fruit and have been pulled up by the roots. They are like wild waves of the sea, churning up the foam of their shameful deeds. They are like wandering stars, doomed forever to blackest darkness. (Jude 1:8–13)

Always be joyful. Never stop praying. Be thankful in all circumstances, for this is God's will for you who belong to Christ Jesus. Do not stifle the Holy Spirit. Do not scoff at prophecies, but test everything that is said. Hold on to what is good. Stay away from every kind of evil. (1 Thessalonians 5:16–22)

Don't be impressed by miracles, signs, wonders, dreams, and visions. Instead keep your eyes on Jesus by standing firmly on His inspired Word. You will know them by their actions and at the center their unconditional love.

> For false messiahs and false prophets will rise up and perform great signs and wonders so as to deceive, if possible, even God's chosen ones. See, I have warned you about this ahead of time. (Matthew 24:24)

Test everything, including all forms of spiritual claims and practices, against the Word of God. If you can't verify it in God's Word, stay away.

> Beware of the false prophets, who come to you in sheep's clothing, but inwardly are ravenous wolves. You will know them by their fruits. Grapes are not gathered from thorn *bushes* nor figs from thistles, are they? So every good tree bears good fruit, but the bad tree bears bad fruit. A good tree cannot produce bad fruit, nor can a bad tree produce good fruit. Every tree that does not bear good fruit is cut down and thrown into the fire. So then, you will know them by their fruits. (Matthew 7:15–19)

Remember, there is *power* in the name of Jesus spoken aloud against our enemies. Say, "In the name of Jesus, the Lord rebuke you, Satan." Moreover, quote Scriptures, pray, and sing worship songs in the face of danger.

CHAPTER 9

God's Promises to Believe

The Bible

> Hear, O Israel! The LORD is our God, the LORD is one! You shall love the LORD your God with all your heart and with all your soul and with all your might. These words, which I am commanding you today, shall be on your heart. You shall teach them diligently to your sons and shall talk of them when you sit in your house and when you walk by the way and when you lie down and when you rise up. You shall bind them as a sign on your hand and they shall be as frontals on your forehead. You shall write them on the doorpost's of your house and on your gates. (Deuteronomy 6:4–9)

> This book of the law shall not depart from your mouth, but you shall meditate on it day and night, so that you may be careful to do according to all that is written in it; for then you will make your way prosperous, and then you will have success. (Joshua 1:8)

> Not one of the good promises which the LORD had made to the house of Israel failed; all came to pass. (Joshua 21:45)

Not one word of all the good words which the LORD your God spoke concerning you has failed; all have been fulfilled for you, not one of them has failed. (Joshua 23:14)

As for God, His way is blameless; the word of the LORD is tried; He is a shield to all who take refuge in Him. (Psalm 18:30)

Your word I have treasured in my heart, that I may not sin against You. Blessed are You, O LORD; teach me Your statutes. (Psalm 119:11–12)

Your word is a lamp to my feet and a light to my path. (Psalm 119:105)

He who gives attention to the word will find good, and blessed is he who trusts in the LORD. (Proverbs 16:20)

Turn to Me and be saved, all the ends of the earth; for I am God, and there is no other. I have sworn by Myself, the word has gone forth from My mouth in righteousness and will not turn back, that to Me every knee will bow, every tongue will swear allegiance. (Isaiah 45:22–23)

For as the rain and the snow come down from heaven, and do not return there without watering the earth and making it bear and sprout, and furnishing seed to the sower and bread to the eater; so will My word be which goes forth from My mouth; it will not return to Me empty, without accomplishing what I desire, and without succeeding in the matter for which I sent it. (Isaiah 55:10–11)

In the beginning was the Word, and the Word was with God, and the Word was God ... The Word became flesh, and dwelt among us, and we saw His glory, glory as of the only begotten from the Father, full of grace and truth. (John 1:1, 14)

Whatever was written in earlier times was written for our instruction, so that through perseverance and the encouragement of the Scriptures we might have hope. (Romans 15:4)

Until I come, give attention to the public reading of Scripture, to exhortation and teaching. (1 Timothy 4:13)

Be diligent to present yourself approved to God as a workman who does not need to be ashamed, accurately handling the word of truth. (2 Timothy 2:15)

From childhood you have known the sacred writings which are able to give you the wisdom that leads to salvation through faith which is in Christ Jesus. All Scripture is inspired by God and profitable for teaching, for reproof, for correction, for training in righteousness; so that the man of God may be adequate, equipped for every good work. (2 Timothy 3:15–17)

The word of God is living and active and sharper than any two-edged sword, and piercing as far as the division of soul and spirit, of both joints and marrow, and able to judge the thoughts and intentions of the heart. (Hebrews 4:12)

No prophecy of Scripture is a matter of one's own interpretation, for no prophecy was ever made by an act of human will, but men moved by the Holy Spirit spoke from God. (2 Peter 1:20–21)

Salvation

Jesus answered and said to him, "Truly, truly, I say to you, unless one is born again he cannot see the kingdom of God." Nicodemus said to Him, "How can a man be born when he is old? He cannot enter a second time into his mother's womb and be born, can he?" Jesus answered, "Truly, truly, I say to you, unless one is born of water and the Spirit he cannot enter into the kingdom of God. That which is born of the flesh is flesh, and that which is born of the Spirit is spirit. Do not be amazed that I said to you, 'You must be born again." (John 3:3–7)

Therefore if anyone is in Christ, he is a new creature; the old things passed away; behold, new things have come. (2 Corinthians 5:17)

He made Him who knew no sin to be sin on our behalf, so that we might become the righteousness of God in Him. (2 Corinthians 5:21)

You were dead in your trespasses and sins. (Ephesians 2:1)

This is good and acceptable in the sight of God our Savior, who desires all men to be saved and to come to the knowledge of the truth. (1 Timothy 2:3–4)

My little children, I am writing these things to you so that you may not sin. And if anyone sins, we have an Advocate with the Father, Jesus Christ the righteous; and He Himself is the propitiation for our sins; and not for ours only, but also for those of the whole world. (1 John 2:1–2)

When you were dead in your transgressions and the uncircumcision of your flesh, He made you alive together with Him, having forgiven us all our transgressions. (Colossians 2:13)

It is a trustworthy statement deserving full acceptance. For it is for this we labor and strive, because we have fixed our hope on the living God, who is the Savior of all men, especially of believers. (1 Timothy 4:9–10)

But the free gift is not like the transgression. For if by the transgression of the one the many died, much more did the grace of God and the gift by the grace of the one Man, Jesus Christ, abound to the many. (Romans 5:15)

Prayer

Ask, and it will be given to you; seek, and you will find; knock, and it will be opened to you. For everyone who asks receives, and he who seeks finds, and to him who knocks it will be opened. (Matthew 7:7–8)

And all things you ask in prayer, believing, you will receive. (Matthew 21:22)

This is the confidence which we have before Him, that, if we ask anything according to His will, He hears us. And if we know that He hears us in whatever we ask, we know that we have the requests which we have asked from Him. (1 John 5:14–15)

Then you will call upon Me and come and pray to Me, and I will listen to you. (Jeremiah 29:12)

It will also come to pass that before they call, I will answer; and while they are still speaking, I will hear. (Isaiah 65:24)

You will pray to Him, and He will hear you; and you will pay your vows. (Job 22:27)

In that day you will not question Me about anything. Truly, truly, I say to you, if you ask the Father for anything in My name, He will give it to you. Until now you have asked for nothing in My name; ask and you will receive, so that your joy may be made full. (John 16:23–24)

Therefore, confess your sins to one another, and pray for one another so that you may be healed. The effective prayer of a righteous man can accomplish much. (James 5:16)

Whatever you ask in My name, that will I do, so that the Father may be glorified in the Son. If you ask Me anything in My name, I will do it. (John 14:13–14)

If you abide in Me, and My words abide in you, ask whatever you wish, and it will be done for you. (John 15:7)

But you, when you pray, go into your inner room, close your door and pray to your Father who is in secret, and your Father who sees what is done in secret will reward you. (Matthew 6:6)

Call upon Me in the day of trouble; I shall rescue you, and you will honor Me. (Psalm 50:15)

Then you will call, and the LORD will answer; You will cry, and He will say, "Here I am." (Isaiah 58:9)

The LORD is far from the wicked, but He hears the prayer of the righteous. (Proverbs 15:29)

He will call upon Me, and I will answer him; I will be with him in trouble; I will rescue him and honor him. (Psalm 91:15)

If you then, being evil, know how to give good gifts to your children, how much more will your Father who is in heaven give what is good to those who ask Him! (Matthew 7:11)

The righteous cry, and the LORD hears and delivers them out of all their troubles. (Psalm 34:17)

Evening and morning and at noon, I will complain and murmur, and He will hear my voice. (Psalm 55:17)

The LORD is near to all who call upon Him, to all who call upon Him in truth. He will fulfill the desire of those who fear Him; He will also hear their cry and will save them. Psalm 145:18–19)

So do not be like them; for your Father knows what you need before you ask Him. (Matthew 6:8)

Whatever we ask we receive from Him, because we keep His commandments and do the things that are pleasing in His sight. (1 John 3:22)

Call to Me and I will answer you, and I will tell you great and mighty things, which you do not know. (Jeremiah 33:3)

Therefore I say to you, all things for which you pray and ask, believe that you have received them, and they will be granted you. (Mark 11:24)

Repentance

For thus the Lord God, the Holy One of Israel, has said, "In repentance and rest you will be saved, in quietness and trust visor strength." (Isaiah 30:15)

Therefore repent and return, so that your sins may be wiped away, in order that times of refreshing may come from the presence of the Lord. (Acts 3:19)

Do you think lightly of the riches of His kindness and tolerance and patience, not knowing that the kindness of God leads you to repentance? (Romans 2:4)

Therefore repent of this wickedness of yours, and pray the Lord that, if possible, the intention of your heart may be forgiven you. (Acts 8:22)

Draw near to God and He will draw near to you. Cleanse your hands, you sinners; and purify your hearts, you double-minded. (James 4:8)

If we confess our sins, He is faithful and righteous to forgive us our sins and to cleanse us from all unrighteousness. (1 John 1:9)

As for me, I baptize you with water for repentance, but He who is coming after me is mightier than I, and I am not fit to remove His sandals; He will baptize you with the Holy Spirit and fire. (Matthew 3:11)

John the Baptist appeared in the wilderness preaching a baptism of repentance for the forgiveness of sins. (Mark 1:4)

I have not come to call the righteous but sinners to repentance. (Luke 5:32)

I tell you that in the same way, there will be more joy in heaven over one sinner who repents than over ninety-nine righteous persons who need no repentance. (Luke 15:7)

Repentance for forgiveness of sins would be proclaimed in His name to all the nations, beginning from Jerusalem. (Luke 24:47)

When they heard this, they quieted down and glorified God, saying, "Well then, God has granted to the Gentiles also the repentance that leads to life." (Acts 11:18)

He is the one whom God exalted to His right hand as a Prince and a Savior, to grant repentance to Israel, and forgiveness of sins. (Acts 5:31)

I now rejoice, not that you were made sorrowful, but that you were made sorrowful to the point of repentance; for you were made sorrowful according to the will of God, so that you might not suffer loss in anything through us. (2 Corinthians 7:9)

For the sorrow that is according to the will of God produces a repentance without regret, leading to salvation, but the sorrow of the world produces death. (2 Corinthians 7:10)

With gentleness correcting those who are in opposition, if perhaps God may grant them repentance leading to the knowledge of the truth. (2 Timothy 2:25)

Therefore leaving the elementary teaching about the Christ, let us press on to maturity, not laying again a foundation of repentance from dead works and of faith toward God. (Hebrews 6:1)

For you know that even afterwards, when he desired to inherit the blessing, he was rejected, for he found no place for repentance, though he sought for it with tears. (Hebrews 12:17)

The Lord is not slow about His promise, as some count slowness, but is patient toward you, not wishing for any to perish but for all to come to repentance. (2 Peter 3:9)

The time is fulfilled, and the kingdom of God is at hand; repent and believe in the gospel. (Mark 1:15)

If the wicked man turns from all his sins which he has committed and observes all My statutes and practices justice and righteousness, he shall surely live; he shall not die. All his transgressions which he has committed will not be remembered against him; because of his righteousness which he has practiced, he will live. (Ezekiel 18:21–22)

Forgiveness

You, Lord, are good, and ready to forgive, And abundant in lovingkindness to all who call upon You. (Psalm 86:5)

"Come now, and let us reason together," Says the LORD, "Though your sins are as scarlet, They will be as white as snow; though they are red like crimson, they will be like wool." (Isaiah 1:18)

Our griefs He Himself bore, and our sorrows He carried; yet we ourselves esteemed Him stricken, smitten of God, and afflicted. But He was pierced through for our transgressions, He was crushed for our iniquities; the chastening for our well-being fell upon Him, and by His scourging we are healed. (Isaiah 53:4–5

"They will all know Me, from the least of them to the greatest of them," declares the LORD, "for I will forgive their iniquity, and their sin I will remember no more." (Jeremiah 31:34)

If you forgive others for their transgressions, your heavenly Father will also forgive you. But if you do not forgive others, then your Father will not forgive your transgressions. (Matthew 6:14–15)

Peter came and said to Him, "Lord, how often shall my brother sin against me and I forgive him? Up to seven times?" Jesus said to him, "I do not say to you, up to seven times, but up to seventy times seven." (Matthew 18:21–22)

This is My blood of the covenant, which is poured out for many for forgiveness of sins. (Matthew 26:28)

Whenever you stand praying, forgive, if you have anything against anyone, so that your Father who is in heaven will also forgive you your transgressions. (Mark 11:25)

In Him we have redemption through His blood, the forgiveness of our trespasses, according to the riches of His grace. (Ephesians 1:7)

Be kind to one another, tender-hearted, forgiving each other, just as God in Christ also has forgiven you. (Ephesians 4:32)

He rescued us from the domain of darkness, and transferred us to the kingdom of His beloved Son, in whom we have redemption, the forgiveness of sins. (Colossians 1:13–14)

When you were dead in your transgressions and the uncircumcision of your flesh, He made you alive together with Him, having forgiven us all our transgressions, having canceled out the certificate of debt consisting of decrees against us, which was hostile to us; and He has taken it out of the way, having nailed it to the cross. (Colossians 2:13–14)

Trust

Offer the sacrifices of righteousness, and trust in the LORD. (Psalm 4:5)

Those who know Your name will put their trust in You, for You, O LORD, have not forsaken those who seek You. (Psalm 9:10)

O my God, in You I trust, do not let me be ashamed; do not let my enemies exult over me. (Psalm 25:20)

I hate those who regard vain idols, but I trust in the LORD. (Psalm 31:6)

As for me, I trust in You, O LORD, I say, "You are my God." (Psalm 31:14)

Our heart rejoices in Him, because we trust in His holy name. (Psalm 33:21)

Trust in the LORD and do good; dwell in the land and cultivate faithfulness. (Psalm 37:3)

Commit your way to the LORD, trust also in Him, and He will do it. (Psalm 37:5)

He put a new song in my mouth, a song of praise to our God; many will see and fear and will trust in the LORD. How blessed is the man who has made the LORD his trust, and has not turned to the proud, nor to those who lapse into falsehood. (Psalm 40:3–4)

I will not trust in my bow, nor will my sword save me. (Psalm 44:6)

As for me, I am like a green olive tree in the house of God; I trust in the lovingkindness of God forever and ever. (Psalm 52:8)

But You, O God, will bring them down to the pit of destruction; men of bloodshed and deceit will not live out half their days. But I will trust in You. (Psalm 55:23)

When I am afraid, I will put my trust in You. In God, whose word I praise, in God I have put my trust; I shall not be afraid. What can mere man do to me? (Psalm 56:3)

Trust in Him at all times, O people; pour out your heart before Him; God is a refuge for us. Do not trust in oppression and do not vainly hope in robbery; if riches increase, do not set your heart upon them. (Psalm 62:8, 10)

Because they did not believe in God and did not trust in His salvation. (Psalm 78:22)

Trust in the LORD with all your heart and do not lean on your own understanding. (Proverbs 3:5)

A wise man scales the city of the mighty and brings down the strong hold in which they trust. (Proverbs 21:22)

So that your trust may be in the LORD, I have taught you today, even you. (Proverbs 22:18)

Trust in the LORD forever, for in GOD the LORD, we have an everlasting Rock. (Isaiah 26:4)

And again, "I will put my trust in Him." And again, "Behold, I and the children whom God has given me." (Hebrews 2:13)

We had the sentence of death within ourselves so that we would not trust in ourselves, but in God who raises the dead. (2 Corinthians 1:9)

I trust that you will realize that we ourselves do not fail the test. (2 Corinthians 13:6)

Suffering

In the day of prosperity be happy, but in the day of adversity consider -- God has made the one as well as the other so that man will not discover anything that will be after him. (Ecclesiastes 7:14)

And not only this, but we also exult in our tribulations, knowing that tribulation brings about perseverance. (Romans 5:3)

If children, heirs also, heirs of God and fellow heirs with Christ, if indeed we suffer with Him so that we may also be glorified with Him. (Romans 8:17)

For to you it has been granted for Christ's sake, not only to believe in Him, but also to suffer for His sake. (Philippians 1:29)

Therefore do not be ashamed of the testimony of our Lord or of me His prisoner, but join with me in suffering for the gospel, according to the power of God. (2 Timothy 1:8)

For you have been called for this purpose, since Christ also suffered for you, leaving you an example for you to follow in His steps. (1 Peter 2:21)

But even if you should suffer for the sake of righteousness, you are blessed. And do not fear their intimidation, and do not be troubled, but sanctify Christ as Lord in your hearts, always being ready to make a defense to everyone who asks you to give an account for the hope that is in you, yet with gentleness and reverence; and keep a good conscience so that in the thing in which you are slandered, those who revile your good behavior in Christ will be put to shame. "For it is better, if God should will it so, that you suffer for doing what is right rather than for doing what is wrong. (1 Peter 3:14–17)

But if anyone suffers as a Christian, he is not to be ashamed, but is to glorify God in this name. (1 Peter 4:16)

After you have suffered for a little while, the God of all grace, who called you to His eternal glory in Christ, will Himself perfect, confirm, strengthen, and establish you. (1 Peter 5:10)

For in the day of trouble He will conceal me in His tabernacle; in the secret place of His tent He will hide me; He will lift me up on a rock. (Psalm 27:5)

That I may know Him and the power of His resurrection and the fellowship of His sufferings, being conformed to His death. (Philippians 3:10)

GOD is our refuge and strength, a very present help in trouble. (Psalm 46:1)

Mercy

But if your enemy is hungry, feed him, and if he is thirsty, give him a drink; for in so doing you will heap burning coals on his head. "o not be overcome by evil, but overcome evil with good. (Romans 12:20–21)

Be merciful, just as your Father is merciful. (Luke 6:36)

What does the LORD require of you but to do justice, to love kindness, and to walk humbly with your God? (Micah 6:8)

He who oppresses the poor taunts his Maker, but he who is gracious to the needy honors Him. (Proverbs 14:31)

Do not let kindness and truth leave you; bind them around your neck, write them on the tablet of your heart. (Proverbs 3:3)

Great are Your mercies, O LORD; revive me according to Your ordinances. (Psalm 119:156)

In all their affliction He was afflicted, and the angel of His presence saved them; in His love and in His mercy He redeemed them, and He lifted them and carried them all the days of old. (Isaiah 63:9)

Therefore, O king, may my advice be pleasing to you: break away now from your sins by doing righteousness and from your iniquities by showing mercy to the poor, in case there may be a prolonging of your prosperity. (Daniel 4:27)

Blessed are the merciful, for they shall receive mercy. (Matthew 5:7)

For He says to Moses, "I will have mercy on whom I have mercy, and I will have compassion on whom I have compassion." (Romans 9:15)

Therefore I urge you, brethren, by the mercies of God, to present your bodies a living and holy sacrifice, acceptable to God, which is your spiritual service of worship. (Romans 12:1)

God, being rich in mercy, because of His great love with which He loved us. (Ephesians 2:4)

Peace

In peace I will both lie down and sleep, For You alone, O LORD, make me to dwell in safety. (Psalm 4:8)

The LORD will give strength to His people; the LORD will bless His people with peace. (Psalm 29:11)

For a child will be born to us, a son will be given to us; and the government will rest on His shoulders; And His name will be called Wonderful Counselor, Mighty God, Eternal Father, Prince of Peace. There will be no end to the increase of His government or of peace, on the throne of David and over his kingdom, to establish it and to uphold it with justice and righteousness from then on and forevermore. The zeal of the LORD of hosts will accomplish this. (Isaiah 9:6–7)

The steadfast of mind You will keep in perfect peace, because he trusts in You. (Isaiah 26:3)

LORD, You will establish peace for us, since You have also performed for us all our works. (Isaiah 26:12)

Peace I leave with you; My peace I give to you; not as the world gives do I give to you. Do not let your heart be troubled, nor let it be fearful. (John 14:27)

Therefore, having been justified by faith, we have peace with God through our Lord Jesus Christ. (Romans 5:1)

The God of peace will soon crush Satan under your feet. The grace of our Lord Jesus be with you. (Romans 16:20)

But now in Christ Jesus you who formerly were far off have been brought near by the blood of Christ. For He Himself is our peace, who made both groups into one and broke down the barrier of the dividing wall. (Ephesians 2:13–14)

Be anxious for nothing, but in everything by prayer and supplication with thanksgiving let your requests be made known to God. And the peace of God, which surpasses all comprehension, will guard your hearts and your minds in Christ Jesus ... The things you have learned and received and heard and seen in me, practice these things, and the God of peace will be with you. (Philippians 4:6–7, 9)

Let the peace of Christ rule in your hearts, to which indeed you were called in one body; and be thankful. (Colossians 3:15)

Despair

We are afflicted in every way, but not crushed; perplexed, but not despairing; persecuted, but not forsaken; struck down, but not destroyed. (2 Corinthians 4:8–9)

Come to Me, all who are weary and heavy-laden, and I will give you rest. Take My yoke upon you and learn from Me, for I am gentle and humble in heart, and you will find rest for your souls. For My yoke is easy and My burden is light. (Matthew 11:28–29)

For His anger is but for a moment, His favor is for a lifetime; weeping may last for the night, but a shout of joy comes in the morning. (Psalm 30:5)

He has not dealt with us according to our sins, nor rewarded us according to our iniquities. For as high as the heavens are above the earth, so great is His lovingkindness toward those who fear Him. As far as the east is from the west, so far has He removed our transgressions from us. (Psalm 103:10–12)

Let us not lose heart in doing good, for in due time we will reap if we do not grow weary. (Galatians 6:9)

Depression

The righteous cry, and the LORD hears and delivers them out of all their troubles. (Psalm 34:17)

He heals the brokenhearted and binds up their wounds. (Psalm 147:3)

Yet those who wait for the LORD will gain new strength; they will mount up with wings like eagles, they will run and not get tired, they will walk and not become weary. (Isaiah 40:31)

Do not fear, for I am with you; do not anxiously look about you, for I am your God. I will strengthen you, surely I will help you, surely I will uphold you with My righteous right hand. (Isaiah 41:10)

When you pass through the waters, I will be with you; and through the rivers, they will not overflow you. When you walk through the fire, you will not be scorched, nor will the flame burn you. (Isaiah 43:2)

For I am convinced that neither death, nor life, nor angels, nor principalities, nor things present, nor things to come, nor powers, nor height, nor depth, nor any other created thing, will be able to separate us from the love of God, which is in Christ Jesus our Lord. (Romans 8:38–39)

Beloved, do not be surprised at the fiery ordeal among you, which comes upon you for your testing, as though some strange thing were happening to you; but to the degree that you share the sufferings of Christ, keep on rejoicing, so that also at the revelation of His glory you may rejoice with exultation. (1 Peter 4:12–13)

So humble yourselves under the mighty power of God, and at the right time he will lift you up in honor. Give all your worries and cares to God, for he cares about you.

Stay alert! Watch out for your great enemy, the devil. He prowls around like a roaring lion, looking for someone to devour. Stand firm against him, and be strong in your faith. Remember that your Christian brothers and sisters all over the world are going through the same kind of suffering you are.

In his kindness God called you to share in his eternal glory by means of Christ Jesus. So after you have suffered a little while, he will restore, support, and strengthen you, and he will place you on a firm foundation. All power to him forever! Amen. 1 Peter 5: 6–11.

There is now no condemnation for those who are in Christ Jesus. (Romans 8:1)

He has not dealt with us according to our sins, nor rewarded us according to our iniquities … As far as the east is from the west, so far has He removed our transgressions from us. (Psalm 103:10, 12)

Therefore if anyone is in Christ, he is a new creature; the old things passed away; behold, new things have come. (2 Corinthians 5:17)

God did not send the Son into the world to judge the world, but that the world might be saved through Him. He who believes in Him is not judged; he who does not believe has been judged already, because he has not believed in the name of the only begotten Son of God. (John 3:17)

Truly, truly, I say to you, he who hears My word, and believes Him who sent Me, has eternal life, and does not come into judgment, but has passed out of death into life. (John 5:24)

For I will be merciful to their iniquities and I will remember their sins no more. (Hebrews 8:12)

I, even I, am the one who wipes out your transgressions for My own sake, and I will not remember your sins. (Isaiah 43:25)

Let the wicked forsake his way and the unrighteous man his thoughts; and let him return to the LORD, and He will have compassion on him, and to our God, for He will abundantly pardon. (Isaiah 55:7)

I acknowledged my sin to You, and my iniquity I did not hide; I said, "I will confess my transgressions to the LORD"; and You forgave the guilt of my sin. (Psalm 32:5)

Then I heard a loud voice in heaven, saying, "Now the salvation, and the power, and the kingdom of

our God and the authority of His Christ have
come, for the accuser of our brethren has been
thrown down, he who accuses them before our
God day and night. And they overcame him
because of the blood of the Lamb and because
of the word of their testimony, and they did
not love their life even when faced with death."
(Revelation 12:10–11)

Stress

Casting all your anxiety on Him, because He
cares for you. (1 Peter 5:7)

No temptation has overtaken you but such as is
common to man; and God is faithful, who will
not allow you to be tempted beyond what you are
able, but with the temptation will provide the way
of escape also, so that you will be able to endure
it. (1 Corinthians 10:13)

Anxiety in a man's heart weighs it down, but a
good word makes it glad. (Proverbs 12:25)

Let your light shine before men in such a way that
they may see your good works, and glorify your
Father who is in heaven. Matthew 5:16)

I will lift up my eyes to the mountains; from
whence shall my help come? My help comes from
the LORD, who made heaven and earth. He will
not allow your foot to slip; He who keeps you will
not slumber. Behold, He who keeps Israel will
neither slumber nor sleep. The LORD is your
keeper; the LORD is your shade on your right
hand. The sun will not smite you by day, nor

the moon by night. The LORD will protect you from all evil; He will keep your soul. The LORD will guard your going out and your coming in from this time forth and forever. (Psalm 121:1–8)

In everything give thanks; for this is God's will for you in Christ Jesus. (1 Thessalonians 5:18)

Be anxious for nothing, but in everything by prayer and supplication with thanksgiving let your requests be made known to God. And the peace of God, which surpasses all comprehension, will guard your hearts and your minds in Christ Jesus. (Philippians 4:6–7)

Peace I leave with you; My peace I give to you; not as the world gives do I give to you. Do not let your heart be troubled, nor let it be fearful. (John 14:27)

God is our refuge and strength, a very present help in trouble. Therefore we will not fear, though the earth should change and though the mountains slip into the heart of the sea; though its waters roar and foam, though the mountains quake at its swelling pride. (Psalm 46:1–3

The LORD also will be a stronghold for the oppressed, a stronghold in times of trouble; and those who know Your name will put their trust in You, for You, O LORD, have not forsaken those who seek You. (Psalm 9:9–10)

CHAPTER 10

Meditate on and Pray the Psalms

Psalm 1:1–6

Oh, the joys of those who do not follow the advice of the wicked, or stand around with sinners, or join in with mockers. But they delight in the law of the LORD, meditating on it day and night. They are like trees planted along the riverbank, bearing fruit each season. Their leaves never wither, and they prosper in all they do. But not the wicked! They are like worthless chaff, scattered by the wind. They will be condemned at the time of judgment. Sinners will have no place among the godly. For the LORD watches over the path of the godly, but the path of the wicked leads to destruction.

Psalm 37

Don't worry about the wicked or envy those who do wrong. For like grass, they soon fade away. Like spring flowers, they soon wither. Trust in the LORD and do good. Then you will live safely in the land and prosper. Take delight in the LORD, and he will give you your heart's desires. Commit everything you do to the LORD. Trust him, and he will help you. He will make your innocence radiate like the dawn, and the justice of your cause will shine like the noonday sun. Be still in the presence of the LORD, and wait patiently for him to act. Don't worry about evil people who prosper in their wicked schemes. Stop being angry! Turn from your rage! Do not lose your temper—it only leads to harm. For the wicked will be destroyed, but those who trust in the LORD will possess the land. Soon the wicked will disappear. Though you look for them, they will be gone. The lowly will possess the land and will live in peace and prosperity. The wicked plot against the godly; they snarl at them in defiance. But the LORD just laughs, for he sees their day of judgment coming. The wicked draw their swords string their bows to kill the poor and the oppressed, to slaughter those who do right. But their swords will stab their own hearts, and their bows will be broken. It is better to be godly and have little than to be evil and rich. but the LORD takes care of the godly. Day by day the LORD takes care of the innocent, and they will receive an inheritance that lasts forever. They will not be disgraced in hard times; even in famine they will have more than enough. But the wicked will die. The LORD's enemies are like flowers in a field—they will disappear like smoke. The wicked borrow and never repay, but the godly are generous givers. Those the LORD blesses will possess the land, but those he curses will die. The LORD directs the steps of the godly. He delights in every detail of their lives. Though they stumble, they will never fall, for the LORD holds them by the hand. Once I was young, and now I am old. Yet I have never seen the godly abandoned or their children begging for bread. The godly always give generous loans to others, and their children are a blessing. Turn from evil and do good, and you will live in the land forever. For the LORD loves justice, and he will never abandon the godly. He will keep them safe forever, but the children of the wicked will die. The godly will possess the land and will live there forever. The godly offer good counsel; they teach right from wrong. They have made God's law their own, so they will never slip from his path. The wicked wait in ambush for the godly, looking for an excuse to kill them. But the LORD will not let the wicked succeed or let the godly be condemned when they are put on trial. Put your hope in the LORD. Travel steadily along his path. He will honor you by giving you the land. You will see the wicked destroyed. I have seen wicked and ruthless People like a tree in its native soil. But when I looked again, they were gone! Though I searched for them, I could not find them! Look at those who are honest and good, for a wonderful future awaits those who love peace. But the rebellious will be destroyed; they have no future. The LORD rescues the godly; he is their fortress in times of trouble. The LORD helps them, rescuing them from the wicked. He saves them, and they find shelter in him.

Psalm 42

As the deer longs for streams of water, so I long for you, OD God. I thirst for God, the living God. When can I go and stand before him? Day and night I have only tears for food, while my enemies continually taunt me, saying, "Where is this God of yours?" My heart is breaking I remember how it used to be: I walked among the crowds of worshipers, leading a great procession to the house of God, singing for joy and giving thanks amid the sound of a great celebration! Why am I discouraged? Why is my heart so sad? I will put my hope in God! I will praise him again—my Savior and my God! Now I am deeply discouraged, but I will remember you— even from distant Mount Hermon, the source of the Jordan, from the land of Mount Mizar. But each day the LORD pours his unfailing love upon me, and through each night I sing his songs, praying to God who gives me life. "O God my rock," I cry, "Why have you forgotten me? Why must I wander around in grief, oppressed by my enemies?" Their taunts break my bones. They scoff, "Where is this God of yours?" Why am I discouraged? Why is my heart so sad? I will put my hope in God! I will praise him again—my Savior and my God!

Psalm 51

Have mercy on me, O God, because of your unfailing love. Because of your great compassion, blot out the stain of my sins. Wash me clean from my guilt. Purify me from my sin. For I recognize my rebellion; it haunts me day and night. Against you, and you alone, have I sinned; I have done what is evil in your sight. You will be proved right in what you say, and your judgment against me is just. For I was born a sinner—yes, from the moment my mother conceived me. But you desire honesty from the womb, teaching me wisdom even there. Purify me from my sins, sins and I will be clean; wash me, and I will be whiter than snow.

Oh, give me back my joy again; you have broken me—now let me rejoice. Don't keep looking at my sins. Remove the stain of my guilt. Create in me a clean heart, O God. Renew a loyal spirit within me. Do not banish me from your presence, and don't take your Holy Spirit from me. Restore to me the joy of your salvation, and make me willing to obey you. Then I will teach your ways to rebels, and they will return to you. Forgive me for shedding blood, O God who saves; then I will joyfully sing of your forgiveness. Unseal my lips, O Lord, that my mouth may praise you. You do not desire a sacrifice, or I would offer one. You do not want a burnt offering. The sacrifice you desire is a broken spirit. You will not reject a broken and repentant heart, O God. Look with favor on Zion and help her; rebuild the walls of Jerusalem. Then you will be pleased with sacrifices offered in the right spirit-with burnt offerings and whole burnt offerings. Then bulls will again be sacrificed on your altar.

Psalm 140 *(Pray this Psalm fervently against our Enemy)*

O Lord, rescue me from evil people. Protect me from those who are violent, those who plot evil in their hearts and stir up trouble all day long.3 Their tongues sting like a snake; the venom of a viper drips from their lips. *Interlude.* O Lord, keep me out of the hands of the wicked. Protect me from those who are violent, for they are plotting against me. The proud have set a trap to catch me; they have stretched out a net; they have placed traps all along the way. *Interlude.* I said to the Lord, "You are my God!" Listen, O Lord, to my cries for mercy! O Sovereign LORD, the strong one who rescued me, you protected me on the day of battle. LORD, do not let evil people have their way. Do not let their evil schemes succeed, or they will become proud. *Interlude.* Let my enemies be destroyed by the very evil they have planned for me. Let burning coals fall down on their heads. Let them be thrown into the fire or into watery pits from which they can't escape. Don't let liars prosper here in our land. Cause great disasters to fall on the violent. But I know the LORD will help those they persecute; he will give justice to the poor. Surely righteous people are praising your name; the godly will live in your presence.

Psalm 91

Those who live in the shelter of the Most High will find rest in the shadow of the Almighty. This I declare about the LORD: He alone is my refuge, my place of safety; he is my God, and I trust him. For he will rescue you from every trap and protect you from deadly disease. He will cover you with his feathers. He will shelter you with his wings. His faithful promises are your armor and protection. Do not be afraid of the terrors of the night, nor the arrow that flies in the day. Do not dread the disease that stalks in darkness, nor the disaster that strikes at midday. Though a thousand fall at your side, though ten thousand are dying around you, these evils will not touch you. Just open your eyes, and see how the wicked are punished. If you make the LORD your refuge, if you make the Most High your shelter, no evil will conquer you; no plague will come near your home. For he will order his angels to protect you wherever you go. They will hold you up with their hands so you won't even hurt your foot on a stone. You will trample upon lions and cobras; you will crush fierce lions and serpents under your feet! The LORD says, "I will rescue those who love me. I will protect those who trust in my name. When they call on me, I will answer; I will be with them in trouble. I will rescue and honor them. I will reward them with a long life and give them my salvation."

Psalm 144

Praise the LORD, who is my rock. He trains my hands for war and gives my fingers skill for battle. He is my loving ally and my fortress, my tower of safety, my rescuer. He is my shield, and I take refuge in him. He makes the nations submit to me. O LORD, what are human beings that you should notice them, mere mortals that you should think about them? For they are like a breath of air; their days are like a passing shadow. Open the heavens, LORD, and come down. Touch the mountains so they billow smoke. Hurl your lightning bolts and scatter your enemies! Shoot your arrows and confuse them! Reach down from heaven and rescue me; rescue me from deep waters, from the power of my enemies. Their mouths are full of lies; they swear to tell the truth, but they lie instead. I will sing a new song to you, O God! I will sing your praises with a ten-stringed harp. For you grant victory to kings! You rescued your servant David from the fatal sword. Save me! Rescue me from the power of my enemies.

Their mouths are full of lies; they swear to tell the truth, but they lie instead. May our sons flourish in their youth like well-nurtured plants. May our daughters be like graceful pillars, carved to beautify a palace. May our barns be filled with crops of every kind. May the flocks in our fields multiply by the thousands, even tens of thousands, and may our oxen be loaded down with produce. May there be no enemy breaking through our walls, no going into captivity, no cries of alarm in our town squares. Yes, joyful are those who live like this! Joyful indeed are those whose God is the LORD.

CHAPTER 11

Worship the Lord

How Are We to Come into the Presence of the Lord?

The answer is found in *Psalm 100*. We are to come before Him with joyful songs, with shouts of joy, and enter His gates with thanksgiving. Praise must be heard. Praise is our verbal and physical response of extolling the Lord. Music, singing, and worship create an atmosphere for miracles.

Remember, when Jesus taught His disciples to pray, His first approach was entering the presence of God with praise. He drew attention to the name of God: "Our Father who is in heaven, hallowed be your name."

> Shout with joy to the LORD, all the earth! Worship the LORD with gladness. Come before him, singing with joy. Acknowledge that the LORD is God! He made us, and we are his. We are his people, the sheep of his pasture. Enter his gates with thanksgiving; go into his courts with praise. Give thanks to him and praise his name. For the LORD is good. His unfailing love continues forever, and his faithfulness continues to each generation. (Psalm 100)

> Give thanks to the LORD and proclaim his greatness. Let the whole world know what he has done. Sing to him; yes, sing his praises. Tell everyone about his wonderful deeds. Exult in his holy name; rejoice, you who worship the LORD. Search for the LORD and for his strength; continually seek him. Remember the wonders he has performed, his miracles, and the rulings he has given, you children of his servant Israel, you descendants of Jacob, his chosen ones. (1 Chronicles 16:8–13)

Worship Songs

Worshiping God through the singing of worship and praise songs is essential in remaining in Him. During my journey and subsequent tribulation, I found it was vital to spend set apart times each day to praise God, whether I felt like it or not. The most important act of worship is singing out loud along with your favorite worship music on radio, CD, or DVD. YouTube is an excellent resource to locate and listen to all your favorites. Simply go to YouTube and enter your favorite worship artist into the search engine. If you're new to all this, ask friends for recommendations of popular worship artist and song titles. I cannot emphasize enough how important it is to draw near to God in praise and worship. Something very intimate and nourishing takes place in our hearts and serves to strengthen us to endure the daily trouble of tribulation. It is vitally important that you use the very tools God has provided. It is not enough to know you should praise and worship God; you must discipline yourself to do it daily and frequently. Try to spend as much time as you can afford praising the King. Below I have listed some popular praise and worship songs. Go to YouTube and enter the song name, along with the artist.

Above All

Above all kingdoms, above all thrones

Above all wonders the world has ever known

Above all wealth and treasures of the earth

There's no way to measure what you're worth

Amazing Grace

Amazing grace! How sweet the sound

That saved a wretch like me!

I once was lost, but now am found

Was blind, but now I see

Amazing Love

I'm forgiven because You were forsaken

I'm accepted, You were condemned

I'm alive and well, Your Spirit lives within me

Because You died and rose again

Another Hallelujah

I love You, Lord, with all my heart

You've given me a brand-new start

And I just want to sing this song to You

It goes like this, the fourth, the fifth

I Can Only Imagine

I can only imagine

What it will be like

When I walk

By your side

Open the Eyes of My Heart

Open the eyes of my heart

Open the eyes of my heart, Lord

Open the eyes of my heart

I want to see You

Here I Am to Worship

Light of the world

You stepped down into darkness.

Opened my eyes, let me see.

Beauty that made this heart adore You

Draw Me Close to You

Draw me close to You

Never let me go

I lay it all down again

To hear You say that I'm Your friend

How Great Is Our God

The splendor of the King,

Clothed in majesty

Let all the earth rejoice

All the earth rejoice

Lord, I Lift Your Name on High

Lord, I lift Your name on high

Lord, I love to sing Your praises

I'm so glad You're in my life

I'm so glad You came to save us

Show Me Your Glory

I caught a glimpse of Your splendor

In the corner of my eye

The most beautiful thing I've ever seen

And it was like a flash of lightning

God of Wonders

Lord of heaven and earth

Lord of all creation

Lord of heaven and earth

Lord of all creation

Singing songs and praising God ranks right up there with prayer. Each draws us closer to Him, and as a result of our worship, He will draw nearer to us. This is good. During this time of tribulation, it would be wise to focus on meditating and studying the Word of God with the focus of knowing everything you can about Him. Please understand it is not enough just to know; you must also obey and apply what the Holy Spirit is teaching you. I recommend times of worship, praise, serving, and loving others, along with Bible training, so you may join Jesus in His work of redeeming the lost. I have written this survival guide to help you have knowledge, wisdom, and practical tools to share your faith and help Jesus share His incredible story.

CHAPTER 12

Communion

The next practice of the devoted follower of Christ is one of the most intimate and mysterious yet essential acts of obedience we take as Christians.

When the time came, Jesus and the apostles sat down together at the table. Jesus said, "I have been very eager to eat this Passover meal with you before my suffering begins. For I tell you now that I won't eat this meal again until its meaning is fulfilled in the Kingdom of God." Then he took a cup of wine and gave thanks to God for it. Then he said, "Take this and share it among yourselves. For I will not drink wine again until the Kingdom of God has come." He took some bread and gave thanks to God for it. Then he broke it in pieces and gave it to the disciples, saying, "This is my body, which is given for you. Do this to remember me." After supper he took another cup of wine and said, "This cup is the new covenant between God and his people—an agreement confirmed with my blood, which is poured out as a sacrifice for you. (Luke 22: 1–20)

The Father allowed His only Son to be substituted in our place on the cross and to take into Himself the full penalty sin required before a perfect and holy and just God. The Father symbolically used Jesus' blood to sign each of our pardons so we could be reconciled to the Father through Jesus' sacrifice. Now whenever you meet together, you should celebrate this amazing grace by remembering the cost of our salvation. We do this by taking the elements of communion—grape juice and unleavened bread— and we look back to the cross and reflect on the graciousness and mercy of our Lord and Savior. Communion is a very sacred act and has a mysterious way of comforting, convicting, and cleansing our hearts. It is wise to take communion often.

God Is Love—the Purpose of Life Is to Learn to Love as Christ

Beloved, let us love one another, for love is from God; and everyone who loves is born of God and knows God. The one who does not love does not know God, for God is love. By this the love of God was manifested in us, that God has sent His only begotten Son into the world so that we might live through Him. In this is love, not that we loved God, but that He loved us and sent His Son *to be* the propitiation for our sins. Beloved, if God so loved us, we also ought to love one another. No one has seen God at any time; if we love one another, God abides in us, and His love is perfected in us. By this we know that we abide in Him and He in us, because He has given us of His Spirit. We have seen and testify that the Father has sent the Son *to be* the Savior of the world. Whoever confesses that Jesus is the Son of God, God abides in him, and he in God. We have come to know and have believed the love which God has for us. God is love, and the one who abides in love abides in God, and God abides in him. By this, love is perfected with us, so that we may have confidence in the day of judgment; because as He is, so also are we in this world. There is no fear in love; but perfect love casts out fear, because fear involves punishment, and the one who fears is not perfected in love. We love, because He first loved us. If someone says, "I love God," and hates his brother, he is a liar; for the one who does not love his brother whom he has seen, cannot love God whom he has not seen. And this commandment we have from Him, that the one who loves God should love his brother also. (1 John 4:7–21)

The Hope of the Resurrection

And now, dear brothers and sisters, we want you to know what will happen to the believers who have died so you will not grieve like people who have no hope. For since we believe that Jesus died and was raised to life again, we also believe that when Jesus returns, God will bring back with him the believers who have died.

We tell you this directly from the Lord: We who are still living when the Lord returns will not meet him ahead of those who have died. For the Lord himself will come down from heaven with a commanding shout, with the voice of the archangel, and with the trumpet call of God. First, the Christians who have died will rise from their graves. Then, together with them, we who are still alive and remain on the earth will be caught

up in the clouds to meet the Lord in the air. Then
we will be with the Lord forever. So encourage
each other with these words. 1 Thessalonians
4:13-18.

Remember those who have gone before. Churchill's speeches
were a great inspiration to the embattled British. His first speech
as prime minister was the famous "I have nothing to offer but
blood, toil, tears, and sweat" speech in which he also said the
following:

> We shall fight in France, we shall fight on the
> seas and oceans, we shall fight with growing
> confidence and growing strength in the air, we
> shall defend our island, whatever the cost may be,
> we shall fight on the beaches, we shall fight on the
> landing grounds, we shall fight in the fields and
> in the streets, we shall fight in the hills; *we shall
> never surrender. Never give in. Never give in. Never,
> never, never, never—in nothing, great or small, large
> or petty—never give in, except to convictions of honor
> and good sense. Never yield to force. Never yield to the
> apparently overwhelming might of the enemy.*

In his other speech he said:

> Let us therefore brace ourselves to our duties, and
> so bear ourselves, that if the British Empire and
> its Commonwealth last for a thousand years, men
> will still say, "This was their finest hour."

You can overcome all things in Christ Jesus. First John 4:4
declares, "He who is in you is greater than he who is in the

world." Remain in *Him*, and fight a good fight. If you take one step, Jesus will take ten for you and others. The stakes are so high. Trust and obey. It's the only way! I love you all. Remain in Christ, and you will be victorious, as the Scriptures promise. Jesus asked,

> Do you finally believe? But the time is coming—indeed it's here now—when you will be scattered, each one going his own way, leaving me alone. Yet I am not alone because the Father is with me. I have told you all this so that you may have peace in me. Here on earth you will have many trials and sorrows. But take heart, because I have overcome the world. (John 16:31–33)

Remain in Jesus, and you too will overcome the world. I have been praying for each of you, and I love you deeply in Christ Jesus our Lord. Keep on!

Christ Our Savior Surely Will Deliver Us

> Now I saw heaven opened, and behold, a white horse. And He who sat on him *was* called Faithful and True, and in righteousness He judges and makes war. His eyes *were* like a flame of fire, and on His head *were* many crowns. He had a name written that no one knew except Himself. He *was* clothed with a robe dipped in blood, and His name is called The Word of God. And the armies in heaven, clothed in fine linen, white and clean, followed Him on white horses. Now out of His mouth goes a sharp sword, that with it He should strike the nations. And He Himself will rule

them with a rod of iron. He Himself treads the winepress of the fierceness and wrath of Almighty God. And He has on *His* robe and on His thigh a name written: KING OF KINGS AND LORD OF LORDS. (Revelation 19:11–16)

Printed in the United States
By Bookmasters